DOOMSDAY KNITS

DOOMSDAY KNITS

Library of Congress Control Number: 2013957515
ISBN 13: 978-1-937513-37-5
Published by www.cooperativepress.com

"Identify Your Apocalypse" Flowchart written by Alexandra Tinsley and illustrated by
Lee DeVito (www.leedevito.com)
Airbrush illustrations courtesy Go Media, Bittbox/Vecteezy.com

FOR COOPERATIVE PRESS

Senior Editor: Shannon Okey
Art Director / Assistant Editor: Elizabeth Green Musselman
Technical Editors: Alexandra Virgiel and Jaya Purswani

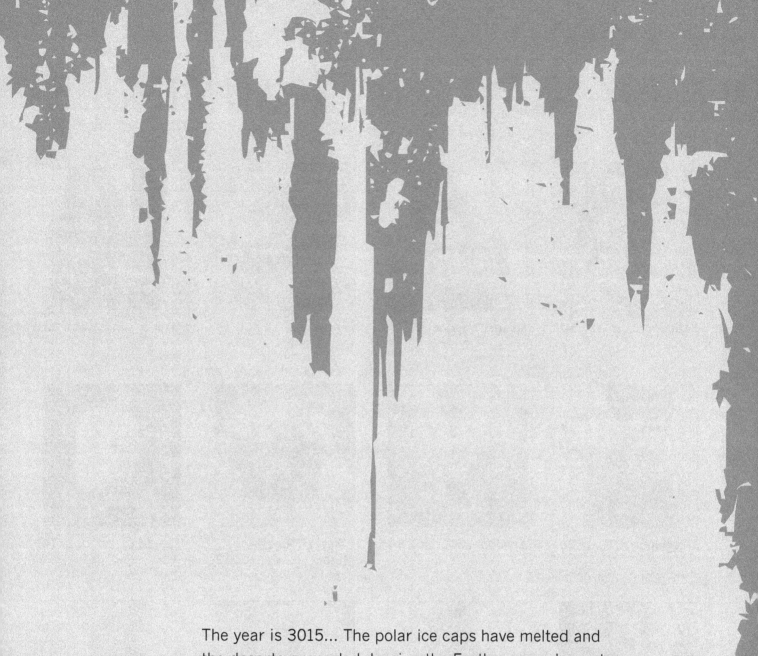

The year is 3015... The polar ice caps have melted and
the deserts expanded, leaving the Earth a seared, crusty
Hell. Meanwhile, nuclear fallout has blocked out the sun,
plunging the world into a new ice age (yes, at the same
time.) While we were distracted by the weather, a race of
intelligent computers enslaved mankind...who have all but
died out thanks to a new, extra virulent virus created by
zombie aliens. Really uptight, controlling zombie aliens,
who spy on us all the time. Oh, and they also drive tricked-
out cars around the desert and wear leather jackets. The
question on your mind?

...

"What should I knit?!"

CONTENTS

Global Warming

It's getting hot in here, so take off all your clothes ... and put these on instead. We DID tell you to lay off the aerosols, did we not?

Situation: The ozone layer is depleted and the ice caps have melted, flooding much of the planet. The rest is largely desert, and boy, is it hot.

FATIGUED

Joanne Scrace

Survivors roam in small groups across the searing desert. Girls rock the sweaty look in sexy military inspired garb, like this low cut, racer back, a-line mini dress with military detailing. Wear with 14-hole Doc Martens and a serious attitude.

PATTERN NOTES

The dress is worked from the top down. The straps are worked flat and then joined to work in the round at the underarm, then later seamed together at the shoulder. Pockets and pocket flaps are knit separately and sewn on. Why not knit one of the large pockets as your gauge swatch?

The dress shown uses jean buttons, which have two parts that snap together and are hammered in place. You can substitute ordinary sew-on buttons, if preferred.

PATTERN

RIGHT FRONT STRAP

CO 8 (8, 10, 10, 12, 12, 14) sts.
Row 1 (RS): Knit.
Row 2: K1, purl to last st, k1.
Work Rows 1 and 2 once more.

Next row (RS): Knit to last 2 sts, kfb, k1.
1 st inc'd.
Next row: K1, purl to last st, k1.

Rep the last 2 rows 9 (11, 11, 13, 14, 16, 17) more times. 18 (20, 22, 24, 27, 29, 32) sts.

Next row: K1, kfb, knit to last 2 sts, kfb, k1. 2 sts inc'd.
Next row: K1, purl to last st, k1.
Rep the last 2 rows four more times. 28 (30, 32, 34, 37, 39, 42) sts.

Place sts onto a stitch holder. Leave yarn attached.

LEFT FRONT STRAP

With a new ball of yarn, CO 8 (8, 10, 10, 12, 12, 14) sts.
Row 1 (RS): Knit.
Row 2: K1, purl to last st, k1.
Work Rows 1 and 2 once more.

Next row (RS): K1, kfb, knit to end. 1 st inc'd.
Next row: K1, purl to last st, k1.
Rep the last 2 rows 9 (11, 11, 13, 14, 16, 17) more times. 18 (20, 22, 24, 27, 29, 32) sts.

Next row (RS): K1, kfb, knit to last 2 sts, kfb, k1. 2 sts inc'd.
Next row: K1, purl to last st, k1.

Rep the last 2 rows 4 more times.
28 (30, 32, 34, 37, 39, 42) sts.

With RS facing, use the cable method to CO 7 sts. 35 (37, 39, 41, 44, 46, 49) sts. Place sts onto a stitch holder. Break yarn.

UPPER BACK

CO 31 (31, 34, 37, 37, 37, 37) sts.
Row 1 (RS): Knit.
Row 2 and all WS rows: K1, purl to last st, k1.
Row 3: [K2, kfb] to last st, k1. 41 (41, 45, 49, 49, 49, 49) sts.
Row 5: Knit.
Row 7: [K3, kfb] to last st, k1. 51 (51, 56, 61, 61, 61, 61) sts.
Row 9: Knit.
Row 11: [K4, kfb] to last st, k1. 61 (61, 67, 73, 73, 73, 73) sts.

Sizes M & L only:
Row 13: Knit.

Sizes XL & 2X only:
Row 13: Knit.
Row 15: [K4, kfb] to last st, k1. – (–, –, –, 85, 85, –) sts.

SIZES

Women's XS (S, M, L, XL, 2X, 3X); shown in size S

Intended to be worn with 1" / 2.5 cm of negative ease at bust.

FINISHED MEASUREMENTS

Bust: 30.5 (33.5, 37.75, 42.25, 46.5, 49.5, 53.75)" / 76.5 (83.5, 94.5, 105.5, 116.5, 123.5, 134.5)cm

MATERIALS

Berroco Remix (30% nylon, 27% cotton, 24% acrylic, 10% silk, 9% linen); 216 yds / 197m per 100g skein); color: Almond (#3903); 4 (4, 5, 5, 6, 7, 8) skeins

32-inch US #8 / 5mm circular needle, or size needed to obtain gauge

Stitch holders, stitch markers, yarn needle, six ¾" / 19mm buttons, sewing needle and thread OR hammer for attaching buttons (see Pattern Notes)

GAUGE

16.5 sts and 21 rows = 4" / 10 cm in St st

Size 3X only:
Row 13: Knit.
Row 15: [K4, kfb] to last st, k1. – (–, –, –, –, –, 85) sts.
Row 17: Knit.

All sizes:
Shape racer back:
BO 17 (17, 19, 20, 19, 19, 19) sts at beg of next 2 rows. 27 (27, 29, 33, 47, 47, 47) sts.
Next row (WS): K1, purl to last st, k1.
Next row (RS): K1, kfb, knit to last 2 sts, kfb, k1. 2 sts inc'd.
Rep the last 2 rows 7 (9, 8, 10, 10, 11, 11) more times, then work WS row once more. 43 (47, 47, 55, 69, 71, 71) sts.

Join fronts and back:
With RS of upper back facing, use the cable method to CO 10 (12, 19, 22, 21, 24, 30) sts. 53 (59, 66, 77, 90, 95, 101) sts. Break yarn. Transfer 35 (37, 39, 41, 44, 46, 49) left front strap sts to left needle with RS facing, then transfer 28 (30, 32, 34, 37, 39, 42) right front strap sts to left needle with RS facing. Using yarn attached to right front strap, use the cable method to CO 10 (12, 19, 22, 21, 24, 30) sts, then knit across all sts, pm and join to work in the round. 126 (138, 156, 174, 192, 204, 222) sts.

BODY

Work 44 (38, 38, 38, 44, 44, 38) rnds even in St st, or until body measures about 8.5 (7.25, 7.25, 7.25, 8.5, 8.5, 7.25)" / 21 (18, 18, 18, 21, 21, 23)cm from underarm.

Next rnd: Remove beg-of-rnd m. K21 (22, 23, 23, 25, 25, 27), pm, [k21 (23, 26, 29, 32, 34, 37), pm] 5 times. Last marker placed is the new beg of rnd.

Dec Rnd: [Knit to 2 sts before m, k2tog, sm] 6 times. 6 sts dec'd.
Rep Dec Rnd on every 6th rnd 1 (2, 2, 2, 2, 2, 3) time(s) more. 114 (120, 138, 156, 174, 186, 198) sts.

Work 5 rnds even.
Inc Rnd: [Knit to 1 st before m, kfb, sm] 6 times. 6 sts inc'd.
Rep Inc Rnd on every 6th rnd 7 (7, 7, 7, 8, 9, 9) times more, then on every 12th rnd twice. 174 (180, 198, 216, 246, 258, 270) sts.

Purl 1 rnd.
Knit 1 rnd.
Purl 1 rnd.
BO all sts kwise.

LARGE POCKET (MAKE 2)

CO 31 sts.
Knit 4 rows.
Next row (WS): K3, purl to last 3 sts, k3.
Next row (RS): Knit.
Rep the last 2 rows 10 more times, then WS row once more.
Knit 4 rows.
BO.

LARGE POCKET FLAP (MAKE 2)

CO 31 sts.
Rows 1–5: Knit.
Row 6 (RS): K4, k2tog, yo, k19, yo, k2tog tbl, k4.
Row 7: Knit.
Row 8: K1, k2tog, knit to last 3 sts, k2tog tbl, k1. 29 sts.
Row 9: Knit.
Row 10: Rep Row 8. 27 sts.
Row 11: Knit.
BO.

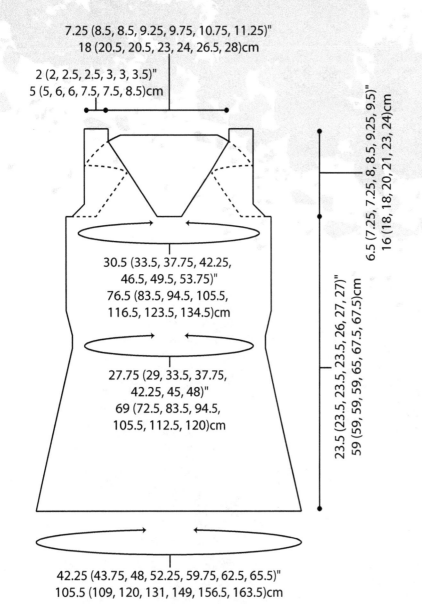

7.25 (8.5, 8.5, 9.25, 9.75, 10.75, 11.25)"
18 (20.5, 20.5, 23, 24, 26.5, 28)cm

2 (2, 2.5, 2.5, 3, 3, 3.5)"
5 (5, 6, 6, 7.5, 7.5, 8.5)cm

30.5 (33.5, 37.75, 42.25, 46.5, 49.5, 53.75)"
76.5 (83.5, 94.5, 105.5, 116.5, 123.5, 134.5)cm

27.75 (29, 33.5, 37.75, 42.25, 45, 48)"
69 (72.5, 83.5, 94.5, 105.5, 112.5, 120)cm

6.5 (7.25, 7.25, 8, 8.5, 9.25, 9.5)"
16 (18, 18, 20, 21, 23, 24)cm

23.5 (23.5, 23.5, 26, 27, 27)"
59 (59, 59, 65, 67.5, 67.5)cm

42.25 (43.75, 48, 52.25, 59.75, 62.5, 65.5)"
105.5 (109, 120, 131, 149, 156.5, 163.5)cm

SMALL POCKET (MAKE 2)

CO 14 sts.
Knit 4 rows.
Next row (WS): K3, p8, k3.
Next row (RS): Knit.
Rep the last 2 rows 4 more times, then
WS row once more.
Next row (RS): K1, k2tog, knit to last 3
sts, k2tog, k1. 2 sts dec'd.
Next row: K3, purl to last 3 sts, k3.
Rep the last 2 rows 3 more times. 6 sts.
Knit 2 rows.
BO.

SMALL POCKET FLAP
(MAKE 2)

CO 14 sts.
Rows 1–5: Knit.

Row 6 (RS): K1, k2tog, knit to last 3 sts,
k2tog, k1. 12 sts.
Row 7: Knit.
Row 8: Rep Row 6. 10 sts.
Row 9: Knit.
Row 10: K1, k2tog, k1, k2tog, yo, k1,
k2tog, k1. 8 sts.
Row 11: Knit.
Row 12: Rep Row 6. 6 sts.
Row 13: Knit.
BO.

FINISHING

Sew shoulder seams.

Neck edging:
With RS facing, beg at bottom of right
front neck, pick up and knit 27 (30, 30,
34, 35, 38, 40) sts up right front neck

edge, 31 (31, 34, 37, 37, 37) sts across
back neck, and 27 (30, 30, 34, 35, 38,
40) sts down left front neck edge. Do not
pick up any sts from the 7-st CO at the
base of the neck. Do not join; work back
and forth in rows.
Knit 5 rows.
BO.
Sew the short ends of the neckband to
the 7-st CO edge, lapping right over left.

Weave in ends. Wet-block all pieces.
Attach buttons to the pockets (two
buttons per large pocket, one button
per small pocket), to correspond with
buttonholes on pocket flaps. Sew
pockets and flaps in place using photo
as a guide.

DESERT WARRIOR

Ellen Gill

When you're part of a nomadic biker tribe, you need protection from the harsh and torrid wastelands. Of course, you need style too. This matching set of gauntlets and legwarmers have a simple yet tough-looking texture that'll fit right in with your leathers. Please note that they cannot guarantee protection from the following: Radioactive snakes, rival biker tribes, explosions.

PATTERN NOTES

Both gauntlets and legwarmers are worked in the round.

GAUNTLET PATTERN

RIGHT GAUNTLET

Forearm:
Using smaller needles, CO 44 sts, pm and join to work in the round. Work in [k1, p1] rib for 8 rnds.

Change to larger needles.
Rnd 1: Work Rnd 1 of Gauntlet Chart over 22 sts, pm, knit to last 2 sts, p2.
Rnds 2–6: Work next rnd of Gauntlet Chart, sm, knit to last 2 sts, p2.
Rnds 7–12: Work next rnd of chart, sm, purl to end.

Rnds 13–24: Rep Rnds 1–12 once.
Rnds 25–29: Rep Rnds 1–5.
Rnd 30: Work in patt to m, sm, ssk, knit to last 4 sts, k2tog, p2. 42 sts.
Rnds 31–36: Rep Rnds 7–12.

Rnds 37–48: Rep Rnds 25–36. 40 sts.
Rnds 49–60: Rep Rnds 1–12.
Rnds 61–66: Rep Rnds 1–6.

Remove second m, leaving beg-of-rnd m in place.

Hand:
Purl 4 rnds.
Knit 3 rnds.

Thumb gusset:
Next rnd: K19, pm, m1, k2, m1, pm, knit to end. 42 sts; 4 sts in thumb gusset.

Knit 3 rnds.
Inc Rnd: Knit to m, sm, m1, knit to next m, m1, sm, knit to end. 2 sts inc'd in thumb gusset.
Rep the last 4 rnds 5 more times. 16 sts in thumb gusset.

Knit 3 rnds.
Next rnd: Knit to m, remove m, sl next 16 sts onto scrap yarn to hold, remove m, CO 2, knit to end. 40 sts.

Knit 4 rnds.
Purl 4 rnds.
BO loosely, pwise.

Thumb:
Return 16 held st to needles. Join yarn, k16, pick up and knit 3 sts from CO edge. 19 sts.

Next rnd: K16, sl 1, k2tog, psso. 17 sts.
Knit 1 rnd.
Purl 4 rnds.
BO loosely, pwise.

LEFT GAUNTLET

Work Forearm and Hand as for right gauntlet.

Thumb gusset:
Next rnd: K1, m1, pm, knit to last st, pm, m1, k1. 42 sts; 4 sts in thumb gusset.

Knit 3 rnds.
Inc Rnd: Knit to m, m1, sm, knit to next m, sm, m1, knit to end.

SIZES

Gauntlets: Women's M (fits knuckle circumference 7–8" / 18–20.5cm)

Legwarmers: Women's M (L) (fits calf circumference 13.5–15 (15–16.5)" / 33.5–37.5 (37.5–41)cm)

Both intended to be worn with 0–2" / 0–5cm of negative ease.

FINISHED MEASUREMENTS

Gauntlet hand circumference: 7.25" / 18cm
Legwarmer calf circumference: 11 (12)" / 27.5 (30)cm
Legwarmer length: approx 20" / 51cm

MATERIALS

Madelinetosh Tosh Merino DK (100% merino wool; 225 yds / 206m per 100g skein); color: Composition Book Grey; 1 skein for gauntlets, 2 skeins for legwarmers

US #6 / 4mm dpns, or size needed to obtain gauge
US #5 / 3.75mm dpns

Stitch marker, yarn needle, scrap yarn

GAUGE

22 sts and 32 rounds = 4" / 10cm in St st, on larger needles

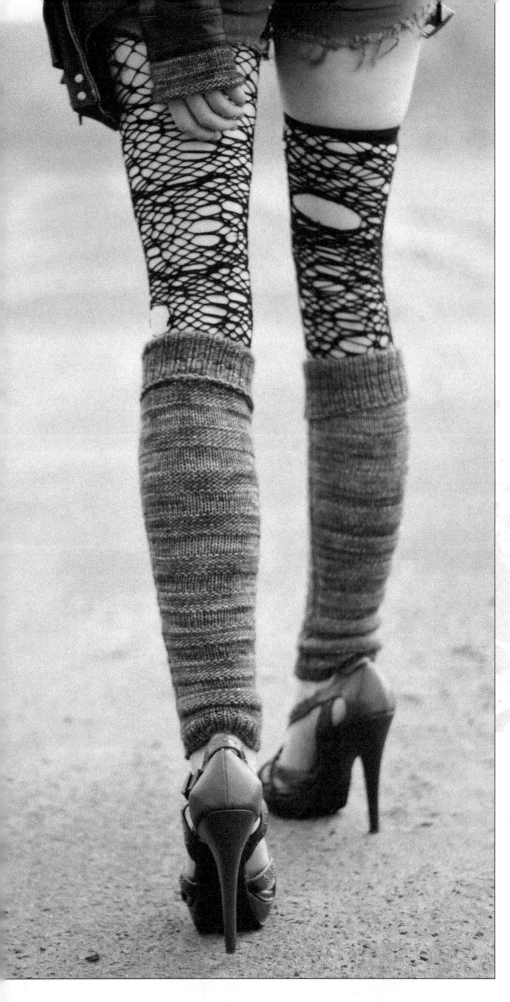

Rep the last 4 rnds 5 more times. 16 sts in thumb gusset.

Knit 3 rnds.
Next rnd: Knit to m, sm, knit to next m, remove m, sl next 16 sts onto scrap yarn to hold, remove m, CO 2. 40 sts.

Knit 4 rnds.
Purl 4 rnds.
BO loosely, pwise.

Work Thumb as for right gauntlet.

FINISHING

Weave in ends. Block by soaking in lukewarm water and drying flat.

LEGWARMER PATTERN

Both legwarmers are worked alike.

BOTTOM CUFF

Using smaller needles, CO 48 (54) sts, pm and join to work in the round. Work in [k1, p1] rib for 8 rnds.

Change to larger needles.

LEG

Rnd 1: Work Rnd 1 of Legwarmer Chart over 26 sts, pm, knit to last 2 sts, p2.
Rnds 2–6: Work next rnd of chart, sm, knit to last 2 sts, p2.
Rnds 7–12: Work next rnd of chart, sm, purl to end.

Rnds 13–36: Rep Rnds 1–12 twice.

Rnd 37: Work in patt to m, sm, m1, knit to last 2 sts, m1, p2. 50 (56) sts.
Rnds 38–41: Rep Rnds 2–5.

Rnd 42: Work in patt to m, sm, m1, knit to last 2 sts, m1, p2. 52 (58) sts.
Rnds 43–48: Rep Rnds 7–12.

Rnds 49–72: Rep Rnds 37–48 twice. 60 (66) sts.
Rnds 73–108: Rep Rnds 1–12 three times.
Next rnd: [K3, k2tog] 12 times, k0 (6). 48 (54) sts.

TOP CUFF

Change to smaller needles. Work in [k1, p1] rib for 20 rnds.

Change to larger needles. Continue in rib for a further 24 rnds.

BO loosely in rib.

FINISHING

Weave in ends. Block by soaking in lukewarm water and drying flat.

GAUNTLET CHART

☐ knit

• purl

☐ pattern repeat

LEGWARMER CHART

FENNEC

Sharon Fuller

The average post-apocalyptic girl so often seems to dress without considering the realities of her environment. This pattern is an attempt to provide clothing appropriate to the arid wasteland without, of course, obscuring anyone's scantily-cladness. The cropped burnoose is worked in a lightweight yarn at a loose gauge for coolness, with a deep hood to protect against glare and sand storms, and a long tail to keep it elegantly secure.

PATTERN NOTES

Garment is knit flat in one piece. Knitting starts at the lower back, works up the back and sleeves, and splits at the neck, with fronts worked separately. Stitches are picked up for the hood. The contrast bands are worked separately and sewn on. The sides and underarms are sewn together.

Since the band, cuffs, sleeves and shoulders increase in width for larger sizes, the sleeve length and bust circumference vary to compensate. Thus, certain measurements and stitch counts may actually decrease from one size to the next larger size.

If you change the sleeve width, you may also wish to adjust the body length accordingly.

STITCHES AND TECHNIQUES

BACKWARD YARN OVER

Instead of wrapping yarn over right needle from front to back, as you would with a regular yo, wrap yarn over right needle from back to front. This uses less yarn and creates a smaller hole than a regular yo.

PATTERN

LOWER BACK

Using US #7 / 4.5mm needle and MC, CO 94 (102, 110, 118, 124, 132, 140, 148) sts. Do not join.

Knit 1 WS row.
Starting with a knit (RS) row, work in St st until piece measures 6.25" / 16cm, ending with a WS row.

BACK SLEEVES

CO 79 (78, 78, 74, 73, 73, 65, 65) sts at beg of next 2 rows. 252 (258, 266, 266, 270, 278, 270, 278) sts.

Work even until sleeves measure 6 (6.25, 6.5, 7, 7.75, 8.75, 9.5, 10.25)" / 15.5 (16, 16.5, 18, 19.5, 22, 24, 26.5)cm from CO, ending with a WS row.

LEFT FRONT

Setup row (RS): Knit 79 (78, 78, 74, 73, 73, 65, 65) right sleeve sts and 24 (28, 32, 36, 39, 43, 47, 51) body sts, then place these 103 (106, 110, 110, 112, 116, 112, 116) sts on scrap yarn. BO next 46 sts for neck, knit to end. 103 (106, 110, 110, 112, 116, 112, 116) sts rem for left side.

Row 1 (WS): Purl.
Row 2: K2, backward yo, k1, backward yo, knit to end. 2 sts inc'd.
Rep Rows 1–2 six more times. 117 (120, 124, 124, 126, 130, 126, 130) sts.

SIZES

Women's XS (S, M, L, XL, 2X, 3X, 4X); shown in size S

Intended to be worn with about 6" / 15cm of positive ease.

FINISHED MEASUREMENTS

Bust: 37 (40, 43, 47.25, 50, 53, 57, 60.25)" / 96 (100, 104, 120.5, 123.5, 137.5, 144, 148)cm, with front bands overlapped

MATERIALS

Elsebeth Lavold Silky Wool (45% wool, 35% silk, 20% nylon; 191 yds / 175m per 50g skein)

⚭ [MC] Wheat #99; 6 (6, 6, 6, 7, 8, 8, 8) skeins

⚭ [CC] Oak #100; 3 (3, 3, 3, 4, 4, 5, 5) skeins

60-inch US #7 / 4.5mm circular needle, or size needed to obtain gauge
60-inch US #6 / 4mm circular needle

60-inch US #5 / 3.75mm circular needle
US size H / 5mm crochet hook

Scrap yarn, stitch marker, yarn needle

GAUGE

20 sts and 28 rows = 4" / 10cm in St st, on US #7 / 4.5mm needle

Work even in St st until sleeve measures 12 (12.5, 13, 14, 15.5, 17.5, 19, 20.5)" / 30 (32, 33, 36, 39, 44, 48, 52)cm from CO, ending with a RS row.

Next row (WS): BO 79 (78, 78, 74, 73, 73, 65, 65) sts, purl to end. 38 (42, 46, 50, 53, 57, 61, 65) sts.

Work even until left front measures 6" / 15.5cm from sleeve BO, or until left front is about 2 rows shorter than back, ending with a WS row.

Purl 1 RS row.
Loosely BO all sts kwise.

RIGHT FRONT

Return 103 (106, 110, 110, 112, 116, 112, 116) sts held sts to needle. Join yarn with WS facing.

Row 1 (WS): Purl.
Row 2: Knit to last 3 sts, backward yo, k1, backward yo, k2. 2 sts inc'd.
Rep Rows 1–2 six more times. 117 (120, 124, 124, 126, 130, 126, 130) sts.

Work even in St st until sleeve measures 12 (12.5, 13, 14, 15.5, 17.5, 19, 20.5)" / 30 (32, 33, 36, 39, 44, 48, 52)cm from CO, ending with a WS row.

Next row (RS): BO 79 (78, 78, 74, 73, 73, 65, 65) sts, knit to end. 38 (42, 46, 50, 53, 57, 61, 65) sts.

Work even until right front measures 6" / 15cm from sleeve BO, or until right front is about 2 rows shorter than back, ending with a WS row.

Purl 1 RS row.
Loosely BO all sts kwise.

HOOD

Using MC and US #7 / 4.5mm needle, with RS facing and beg at base of right front neck shaping, pick up and knit 14 sts from right front edge, 46 sts across back neck, and 14 sts down left front edge to base of neck shaping. 74 sts.

Beg with a WS row, work even in St st until hood measures 13.5" / 34.5cm, ending with a WS row. On last row, pm at center back (37 sts on either side of marker).

Shape top:
Row 1 (RS): Knit to 2 sts before m, ssk, sm, k2tog, knit to end. 2 sts dec'd.
Row 2 and all WS rows: Purl.

Row 3: Rep Row 1. 70 sts.

Row 5: Knit to 7 sts before m, ssk, k3, ssk, sm, k2tog, k3, k2tog, knit to end. 66 sts.

Row 7: Knit to 6 sts before m, ssk, k2, ssk, sm, k2tog, k2, k2tog, knit to end. 62 sts.
Row 9: Knit to 8 sts before m, [ssk, k1] twice, ssk, sm, k2tog, [k1, k2tog] twice, knit to end. 56 sts.

Row 11: Knit to 6 sts before m, [ssk] 3 times, remove m, [k2tog] 3 times, knit to end. 50 sts.
Divide sts evenly over two needles and join with a 3-needle BO on WS.

CUFFS (MAKE 2)

Chart patt is worked over a mult of 8 sts plus 2 selvage sts. Progressively smaller needles are used to control gauge as the stitch patt becomes more open.

Using CC and US #7 / 4.5mm needle, CO 58 (66, 66, 74, 82, 90, 98, 106) sts.

** Beg with Row 5 (5, 5, 5, 5, 5, 1, 1), work Edging Chart through Row 12.

Change to US #6 / 4mm needle. Work chart from Row 13 through Row 22 (22, 22, 22, 22, 22, 26, 26).

Change to US #5 / 3.75mm needle. Rep Rows 27–28 of chart until cuff measures 4 (4, 4, 5, 5, 5, 6, 6)" / 10 (10, 10, 12.5, 12.5, 12.5, 15, 15)cm, or desired length, ending with Row 27.

Using US #7/ 4.5mm needle, loosely BO all sts kwise on WS.**

BAND

Using CC and US #7 / 4.5mm needle, CO 442 (442, 458, 466, 482, 506, 514, 538) sts. Work as for Cuffs from ** to **.

Note that tail ends of band tend to stretch quite a bit, so you may want to take that into account when choosing how many sts to CO.

FINISHING

Block body to schematic measurements. Block cuffs to 12 (12.5, 13, 14, 15.5, 17.5, 19, 20.5)" / 30 (32, 33, 36, 39, 44, 48, 52)cm wide by 4 (4, 4, 5, 5, 5, 6, 6)" / 10 (10, 10, 12.5, 12.5, 12.5, 15, 15) cm long, and band to 88.5 (88.5, 91.5, 93.25, 96.5, 101.25, 102.75, 107.5)" / 221 (221, 229, 233, 241, 253, 257, 269) cm wide by 4 (4, 4, 5, 5, 5, 6, 6)" / 10 (10, 10, 12.5, 12.5, 12.5, 15, 15)cm long.

Using CC and crochet hook, with WS facing work a stabilizing row of slip stitch along the neckline/hood pick-up line. (Crochet sts should not show on RS.)

Sew cuffs to ends of sleeves.
Sew side and sleeve seams.

Sew band around front opening, one end flush with bottom edge of garment, other end with approx 32.5 (32, 34.5, 35, 37, 40, 40, 43)" / 82 (82, 88, 89, 94, 101, 101, 109)cm hanging free. (Garment pictured has tail on right side.)

EDGING CHART

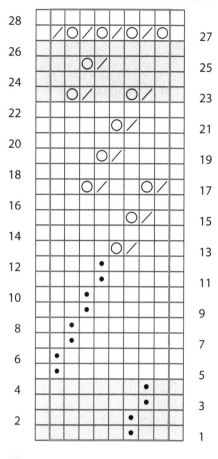

	RS: knit; WS: purl
•	RS: purl; WS: knit
○	yo
/	k2tog
	pattern repeat

Work shaded rows for sizes 3X and 4X only. For all other sizes, skip these rows.

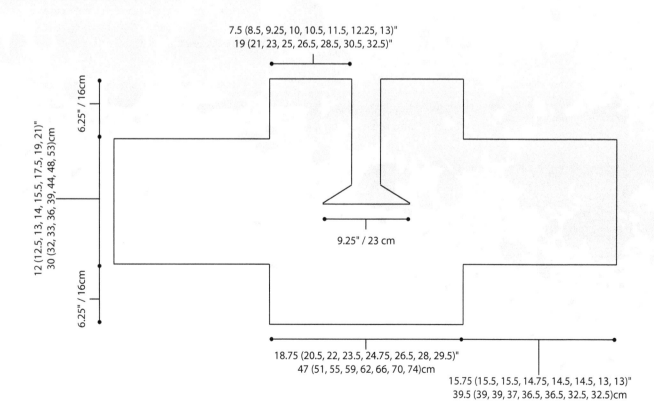

7.5 (8.5, 9.25, 10, 10.5, 11.5, 12.25, 13)"
19 (21, 23, 25, 26.5, 28.5, 30.5, 32.5)"

6.25" / 16cm

6.25" / 16cm

12 (12.5, 13, 14, 15.5, 17.5, 19, 21)"
30 (32, 33, 36, 39, 44, 48, 53)cm

9.25" / 23 cm

18.75 (20.5, 22, 23.5, 24.75, 26.5, 28, 29.5)"
47 (51, 55, 59, 62, 66, 70, 74)cm

15.75 (15.5, 15.5, 14.75, 14.5, 14.5, 13, 13)"
39.5 (39, 39, 37, 36.5, 36.5, 32.5, 32.5)cm

OZONE

Rebecca Zicarelli

After the apocalypse, there will be no one to tell you you're knitting the wrong way. Time is precious and the efficient knitter wraps stitches as they're needed in the next row to eliminate the need for the "slip, slip" part of the SSK; a technique today's knitters call combined knitting. Ozone (which is both a layer and full of holes) uses a lot of slip-slipping, so consider this a skill-building meditation in controlling how you wrap your stitches and speeding your knitting. The zig-zagging lace pattern lacks straight lines that might attract the human eye, providing camouflage that you can peek through easily. The fringed bottom, in a lighter-weight yarn for maximum movement, is essential for softening the line between where you end and the sand begins.

STITCHES AND TECHNIQUES

VERTICAL LACE TRELLIS

(Worked in the round, mult of 2 sts + 1)
Rnd 1: Knit.
Rnd 2: [K2tog, yo] to last st, k1.
Rnd 3: Knit.
Rnd 4: K1, [yo, ssk] to end.
Rep Rnds 1–4.

COMBINED KNITTING

A stitch has two legs: one leg over the front of the needle, the other over the back. In standard Western knitting, we always wrap the yarn so that when we encounter the stitch on the following row, its leading leg is forward and its trailing leg is in back. When we k2tog with the stitches mounted this way, it creates a right-leaning decrease. To make a left-leaning decrease, we work an ssk, slipping the two stitches knitwise, on at a time, to reverse the stitch mount and bring the trailing leg forward before we knit them together.

In combined knitting, the yarn is wrapped based on how the stitches will be used in the following row. Standard wrapping wraps from the front of the needle over the top to the back. Wrapping the yarn the other way, from back to front, mounts the stitches with the trailing leg forward. Wrapping back-to-front eliminates the need to slip stitches for an ssk*, and greatly speeds the knitting. Combining both ways of wrapping is called combined knitting.

The lace pattern is worked over four rounds: first pattern rnd, plain rnd, second pattern rnd, plain rnd. Half of each pattern rnd will be worked as [k2tog, yo], and the other half will be [yo, ssk]. On the plain rnds, you can wrap the stitches the standard way (front to back, leading leg forward) for the half of the shawl that will be [k2tog, yo] in the next rnd; for the half that will be [yo, ssk], wrap the opposite way (back to front, trailing leg forward). The rnds are short at first, so that it's easy to tink back if you make a mistake, then they get longer as you gain proficiency. There will be one stitch at the beginning of each [yo, ssk] half that is not knit with another stitch in a decrease; avoid twisting it; knit the leading leg, which is in the back of the needle, not the trailing leg, which will be to the front.

*To work an ssk on sts mounted with the trailing leg forward, insert the right needle into the next 2 sts from right to left and knit them together.

SIZES

Regular (Tall); shown in Tall

Regular fits folks up to 5'6". Tall is for supermodels and Zombie Warriors of the future.

FINISHED MEASUREMENTS

Center back length: 34 (38)" / 86.5 (96.5)cm

MATERIALS

[MC] Quince & Co. Osprey (100% wool, 170 yds / 155m per 100g skein); color: Chanterelle; 5 (6) skeins

[CC] Quince & Co. Chickadee (100% wool, 181 yds / 166m per 50g skein); color: Chanterelle; 2 skeins

24-inch US #10 / 6mm circular needle, or size needed to obtain gauge

40-inch US #10 / 6mm circular needle

Stitch markers, including 1 locking marker, crochet hook for applying fringe, yarn needle

GAUGE

10 sts and 14 rows = 4" / 10cm in St st with MC

PATTERN NOTES

Ozone begins with a figure-eight cast on, which provides stitches going in either direction for the beginning of the neckband and a center-back triangular base. When the base is complete, the neckband is worked back and forth as a long strip with a miter at center front neck, then grafted to the other end of the band to form a circle. Stitches are picked up from the long edge of the neckband, added to the sts of the center-back triangle, and work proceeds in the round with increases at center front and center back.

The center-back and center-front stitches will have a marker and a yarn over on each side; take care that the markers remain next to the center stitches and don't migrate outward into the work like thoughtless zombies.

The fringe is made with light sport-weight yarn in the same color, to increase fullness and movement. If you prefer, you can fringe with single strands of MC instead of double strands of CC, in which case you will require an extra skein of the Osprey and no Chickadee.

PATTERN

FIGURE-EIGHT CAST ON

Hold shorter circular needle with the points parallel and both pointing to the left. With MC, make a backward loop over the bottom needle, and then hold the yarns in a V in your left hand, as if working a long-tail cast on, with the ball end over the index finger for the top strand and the tail over the thumb for the bottom strand, both strands tensioned in the palm of your hand. Bring the top needle into the middle of the V and under the bottom strand of yarn, making one stitch on the top needle. *Bring the bottom needle above

the V and under the top strand of yarn and up through the V; top needle into the V and under the bottom strand. Repeat from * once. There will be three stitches on each needle. Pull the working yarn between the needles so that everything feels snug, and the gently pull bottom needle though the stitches on it so that they float on the cable, freeing the needle to work. Flip the work over; you should see the line of purl bumps between the three stitches on the needles and the three stitches floating on the cable.

NECKBAND AND BACK BASE

Row 1 (RS): K3, slide the 3 sts on the cable onto the left-hand needle, yo, k3. 7 sts.
Row 2: K3, yo, pm, k1 (this is the center back st), pm, yo, k3. 9 sts.
Row 3: K3, p1, sm, p1, sm, p1, k3.
Row 4: K3, yo, k1, yo, sm, k1, sm, yo, k1, yo, k3. 13 sts.

Row 5: K3, pm, p3, sm, p1, sm, p3, sm, k3.
Row 6: K3, sm, yo, knit to m, yo, sm, k1, sm, yo, knit to m, yo, sm, k3. 4 sts inc'd.
Row 7: K3, sm, purl to m, sm, p1, sm, purl to m, sm, k3.
Rep Rows 6–7 four more times. 33 sts.

Next row (RS): K3, sm, yo, knit to m, yo, sm, k1, sm, yo, knit to m, yo, sm, k1, kfb, k1. 38 sts.
38 sts in total: Viewed from RS, 3 neckband sts, marker, 15 St sts, marker, 1 center back st, marker, 15 St sts, marker, 4 neckband sts.

Work neckband:
This section is worked over the first 4 sts only. Leave the rest of the sts on the needle but ignore them for now.
Row 1 (WS): K4, turn.
Row 2: Sl 1 wyif, k3.
Rep these 2 rows 18 more times; there should be 19 slipped sts along the edge of the band.

Work 4-row miter:
Row 1 (WS): Knit.
Row 2: Sl 1 wyif, k1, w&t.
Row 3: K2.
Row 4: Sl 1 wyif, k3.

Next row (WS): K4, turn.
Next row: Sl 1 wyif, k3. Place locking marker in the slipped stitch to mark center front of neckband.
Work the 4-row miter again.

Next row: (WS): K4, turn.
Next row: Sl 1 wyif, k3.
Rep the last 2 rows 18 more times. There should be 19 slipped sts along the neckband edge, counting from the center front.

Next row (WS): K1, k2tog, k1. 3 sts. Break yarn leaving a 12" / 30cm tail. Make sure the band is not twisted, then use the tail to graft these neckband sts to the 3 neckband sts on the opposite end of the needle.

BODY

Note: Read the following section carefully before proceeding; poncho uses a special pick-up method that results in a row of lace holes separating neckband from body of the poncho and allows for more stretch to get the band over your head.

With RS facing, using shorter needle and beginning at left edge of back panel, pick up 20 sts along the neckband by picking up the public-side leg of each slipped stitch. Don't pick up and knit, and don't pick up the back leg of the stitch. Pm, remove the locking marker at center front and pick up the marked st. Pm, and in the same way pick up the next 20 sts from the band. Slip the next 15 sts and the following marker to the right needle. You should now be at center back; rounds will begin at this point from now on.

72 sts in total: 1 center back st, marker, 35 St st/picked-up sts, marker, 1 center front st, marker, 35 St st/picked-up sts, marker.

Join MC.
Rnd 1: K1, sm, knit to m, sm, k1, sm, knit to m wrapping back to front (see Combined Knitting), sm.

Rnd 2: K1, sm, yo, [k2tog, yo] to 1 st before m, k1, yo, sm, k1, sm, yo, k1, [yo, ssk] to m (see Combined Knitting), yo, sm. 4 sts inc'd.

Rnd 3: K1, sm, knit to m wrapping back to front, sm, k1, sm, knit to m, sm.

Rnd 4: K1, sm, yo, k1, [yo, ssk] to m, yo, sm, k1, sm, yo, [k2tog, yo] to 1 st before m, k1, yo, sm. 4 sts inc'd.

Changing to longer needle when necessary, rep Rnds 1–4 25 (28) more times, until you have 280 (304) sts, until work measures 33 (37)" / 84 (94)cm at center back, or until you've used up 4 (5) skeins of yarn, as you prefer.
Knit 1 rnd.

Bottom edging:
Rnd 1: K1, sm, yo, purl to m, yo, sm, k1, sm, yo, purl to m, yo, sm. 4 sts inc'd.
Rnd 2: Knit.
Rep these 2 rnds twice more.
Using 2 strands of MC held together, BO all sts loosely.

FINISHING

Weave in ends. Steam block the opening and bottom edge, stretching them open. Lace body does not require blocking.

Using crochet hook, attach fringe around the bottom using two 13" / 33cm strands of CC in each bound-off st. The easiest way to cut the strands is to wrap the yarn in a single layer around a book 6.5" / 16.5cm wide; I used the sacred tome *Green Eggs and Ham*. Cut using the space between the covers as a guide to keep your line straight and your strands an even length.

OXYGENATE

Melissa Lemmons

In a world covered by water, humans fight for survival. The polar ice caps have melted, leaving little dry land. Bio-engineered humans have adapted by incorporating gills into their anatomy. This laceweight tank is cool in the wasteland of water and sun and stylishly accents the gills while allowing ease of movement. The lace pattern mimics the scales of the fish they swim with.

STITCHES AND TECHNIQUES

K1E – KNIT 1 ELONGATED

Knit, wrapping yarn twice around needle. On following row, drop the extra wrap.

PATTERN NOTES

This sleeveless tank is worked from the bottom up. It starts in the round until just before the armholes when short rows are used to set up for the pleated panels. The short rows are continued after splitting for the armholes. After short rows are worked on both sides of the front, the pleated panels and center triangle are worked all at once in full rows, using intarsia. Then short rows are used again to fill in the space above the pleated panels and the shoulders are

finished off by working back and forth. The back is worked back and forth then the shoulder seams are grafted together.

Silk yarn grows when blocked, so for best results be sure to knit a large swatch and block it before beginning the tank.

When as a result of shaping there are not enough sts to work both a yo and its corresponding dec together in the lace pattern, work the extra sts in St st.

PATTERN

BODY

With MC, CO 228 (240, 264, 276, 300, 312) [324, 348, 360, 372, 396, 408] {420, 444, 456, 480, 492, 504} sts. Pm and join to work in the round.

Work in garter st (knit 1 rnd, purl 1 rnd) for 6 rnds.

Work Rnds 1–8 of Lace chart 20 times.

Sizes 30.5 (32, 35.25, 36.75, 40, 41.5) [43.25, 46.5, 48, 49.5, 52.75, 54.5] {–, –, –, –, –, –} only:
Short row 1 (RS): K3, work in lace patt to last 29 sts of rnd, w&t.
Short row 2 (WS): Work in patt to last 4 sts of rnd, w&t.

Short row 3: K3, work in patt to 3 sts before previous wrapped st, w&t.
Short row 4: Work in patt to 3 sts before previous wrapped st, w&t.
Rep Short Rows 3–4 1 (1, 0, 0, 0, 0) [0, 0, 0, 0, 0, 0] {–, –, –, –, –, –} more time(s).

Sizes – (–, –, –, –, –) [–, –, –, –, –, –] {56, 59.25, 60.75, 64, 65.5, 67.25}" only:
Short row 1 (RS): K3, work in lace patt to last 29 sts of rnd, w&t.
Short row 2 (WS): Work in patt to last 4 sts of rnd, w&t.

SIZES

To fit bust 28 (30, 32, 34, 36, 38) [40, 42, 44, 46, 48, 50] {52, 54, 56, 58, 60, 62}" / 70 (76, 81.5, 96.5, 91.5, 96.5) [101.5, 106.5, 112, 117, 122, 127] {132, 137, 142, 147.5, 152.5, 157.5}cm; shown in size to fit 30" / 76cm

Intended to be worn with 2.5–5.5" / 5–14cm of positive ease.

FINISHED MEASUREMENTS

Bust: 30.5 (32, 35.25, 36.75, 40, 41.5) [43.25, 46.5, 48, 49.5, 52.75, 54.5] {56, 59.25, 60.75, 64, 65.5, 67.25}" / 76 (80, 88, 92, 100, 104) [108, 116, 120, 124, 132, 136] {140, 148, 152, 160, 164, 168}cm

MATERIALS

[MC] The Unique Sheep Marici (100% silk; 1250 yds / 1143m per 114g skein); color: Supernova 3; 1 (1, 1, 1, 1, 1) [1, 1, 1, 1, 1, 1] {1, 2, 2, 2, 2, 2} skeins

[CC] The Unique Sheep Chasca (100% alpaca; 1250 yds / 1134m per 114g skein); color: Supernova 5; 1 skein

32-inch US #2 / 2.75mm circular needle, or size needed to obtain gauge

Stitch markers, stitch holders or waste yarn, yarn needle

GAUGE

30 sts and 48 rnds = 4" / 10cm in Lace patt with MC, blocked

30 sts and 43 rows = 4" / 10cm in St st with MC, blocked

LACE CHART

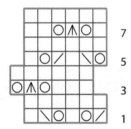

To work Rnd 3: Remove beg-of-rnd m, sl first st, pm, work as charted to end of rnd.

Return m to original position on Rnd 4: Work to last st of rnd, sl last st, remove m, return slipped st to left needle, pm.

☐ knit

○ yo

╲ ssk

╱ k2tog

⋀ sl 2 as if to k2tog, k1, p2sso

☐ pattern repeat

All sizes:

Divide for armholes (RS): K3, work 28 (31, 38, 41, 45, 48) [51, 55, 58, 61, 65, 68] {73, 78, 81, 85, 88, 91} sts in patt then place these 31 (34, 41, 44, 48, 51) [54, 58, 61, 64, 68, 71] {76, 81, 84, 88, 91, 94} sts on holder for right front, BO 7 (7, 11, 11, 15, 15) [15, 19, 19, 19, 23, 23] {25, 27, 27, 31, 31, 31} sts using a stretchy method, work 107 (113, 121, 127, 135, 141) [147, 155, 161, 167, 175, 181] {185, 195, 201, 209, 215, 221} sts in patt then place these sts on holder for back, BO 7 (7, 11, 11, 15, 15) [15, 19, 19, 19, 23, 23] {25, 27, 27, 31, 31, 31} sts using a stretchy method, work in patt to 3 sts before previous wrapped st, w&t.

Left Front short rows:

Next row (WS): Purl to last 3 sts, k1, sl 1 wyif, p1.
Next row (RS): Sl 1 wyib, k1e, p1, [ssk] twice, work in patt to 3 sts before previous wrapped st, w&t. 2 sts dec'd at armhole edge.

Rep the last 2 rows 2 (2, 3, 4, 6, 6) [6, 8, 8, 8, 10, 11] {10, 12, 12, 14, 14, 14} more times.

Next row (WS): Purl to last 3 sts, k1, sl 1 wyif, p1.

Next row (RS): Sl 1 wyib, k1e, p1, ssk, work in patt to 3 sts before previous wrapped st, w&t. 1 st dec'd at armhole edge.
Next row (WS): Purl to last 3 sts, k1, sl 1 wyif, p1.
Rep the last 2 rows 1 (2, 2, 2, 0, 1) [2, 0, 1, 2, 0, 0] {2, 1, 2, 0, 1, 2} more time(s).

All sizes:
Cut yarn. Leave sts on needle.

Right Front short rows:

Place 31 (34, 41, 44, 48, 51) [54, 58, 61, 64, 68, 71] {76, 81, 84, 88, 91, 94} sts from holder onto needle that already contains the sts from the left and center front. Join MC with WS facing.

Next row (WS): P1, sl 1 wyif, k1, purl to 3 sts before previous wrapped st, w&t.

Next row (RS): K3, work in patt to last 7 sts, [k2tog] twice, p1, k1e, sl 1 wyib. 2 sts dec'd at armhole edge.
Next row (WS): P1, sl 1 wyif, k1, purl to 3 sts before previous wrapped st, w&t.
Rep the last 2 rows 2 (2, 3, 4, 6, 6) [6, 8, 8, 8, 10, 11] {10, 12, 12, 14, 14, 14} more times.

Next row (RS): K3, work in patt to last 5 sts, k2tog, p1, k1e, sl 1 wyib. 1 st dec'd at armhole edge.
Next row (WS): P1, sl 1 wyif, k1, purl to 3 sts before previous wrapped st, w&t.
Rep the last 2 rows 1 (2, 2, 2, 0, 1) [2, 0, 1, 2, 0, 0] {2, 1, 2, 0, 1, 2} more time(s).

All sizes:
Cut yarn. Leave sts on needle.

After all left front and right front short rows and armhole decreases have been worked, 91 (95, 99, 101, 105, 109) [113, 117, 121, 125, 129] {131, 135, 139, 143, 147, 151, 155} front sts rem.

PLEATED GILLS

These rows are worked across the whole front. Divide CC into two balls before starting. CC is used for each of the pleated panels on each side and MC is used for the center triangle, using intarsia techniques. Make sure to bring the new yarn up from under the old yarn when switching colors, to prevent holes.

Note: As you work Row 1, pick up and knit wraps tog with wrapped sts.

Row 1 (RS): Join CC. With CC, sl 1 wyib, k1e, p1, k3 (5, 1, 2, 4, 6) [2, 4, 6, 2, 4, 5] {1, 3, 5, 1, 3, 5}, pm, [use the backward loop method to CO 5 sts, k6] 4 (4, 5, 5, 5) [6, 6, 6, 7, 7, 7] {8, 8, 8, 9, 9, 9} times, CO 5 sts, k3; join MC, work 25 sts in lace patt in MC; join second ball of CC, k3, CO 5 sts, [k6, CO 5 sts] 4 (4, 5, 5, 5) [6, 6, 6, 7, 7, 7] {8, 8, 8, 9, 9, 9} times, pm, k3 (5, 1, 2, 4, 6) [2, 4, 6, 2, 4, 5] {1, 3, 5, 1, 3, 5}, p1, k1e, sl 1 wyib.

Row 2 and all WS rows through Row 18: With CC, p1, sl 1 wyif, k1, purl to end of first CC section; work to end of MC section with MC; purl to last 3 sts of second CC section, k1, sl 1 wyif, p1.

Row 3: With CC, sl 1 wyib, k1e, p1, m1, knit to m, sm, [sl 1 wyib, k2, p1, k7] 4 (4, 5, 5, 5) [6, 6, 6, 7, 7, 7] {8, 8, 8, 9, 9, 9} times, sl 1 wyib, k2, p1, k5; with MC, sssk, work in patt to last 3 MC sts, k3tog; with CC, k5, p1, k2, sl 1 wyib, [k7, p1, k2, sl 1 wyib] 4 (4, 5, 5, 5) [6, 6, 6, 7, 7, 7] {8, 8, 8, 9, 9, 9} times, sm, knit to last 3 sts, m1, p1, k1e, sl 1 wyib. 2 sts inc'd and 4 sts dec'd for a net reduction of 2 sts.

Row 5: Rep Row 3.

Row 7: With CC, sl 1 wyib, k1e, p1, m1, knit to m, sm, [sl 1 wyib, k2, p1, k7] 4 (4, 5, 5, 5) [6, 6, 6, 7, 7, 7] {8, 8, 8, 9, 9, 9} times, sl 1 wyib, k2, p1, k5; with MC, work in patt to end of MC sts; with CC, k5, p1, k2, sl 1 wyib, [k7, p1, k2, sl 1 wyib] 4 (4, 5, 5, 5) [6, 6, 6, 7, 7, 7] {8, 8, 8, 9, 9, 9} times, sm, knit to last 3 sts, m1, p1, k1e, sl 1 wyib. 2 sts inc'd.

Row 9: Rep Row 3.
Row 11: Rep Row 7.
Row 13: Rep Row 3.
Row 15: Rep Row 3.

Row 17: With CC, sl 1 wyib, k1e, p1, m1, knit to m, sm, [sl 1 wyib, k2, p1, k7] 4 (4, 5, 5, 5) [6, 6, 6, 7, 7, 7] {8, 8, 8, 9, 9, 9} times, sl 1 wyib, k2, p1, k5; with MC, ssk, k1, k2tog; with CC, k5, p1, k2, sl 1 wyib, [k7, p1, k2, sl 1 wyib] 4 (4, 5, 5, 5) [6, 6, 6, 7, 7, 7] {8, 8, 8, 9, 9, 9} times, sm, knit to last 3 sts, m1, p1, k1e, sl 1 wyib. 2 sts inc'd and 2 sts dec'd; no change to st count.

Row 19: With CC, sl 1 wyib, k1e, p1, m1, knit to m, sm, [sl 1 wyib, k2, p1, k7] 4 (4, 5, 5, 5) [6, 6, 6, 7, 7, 7] {8, 8, 8, 9, 9, 9} times, sl 1 wyib, k2, p1, k5; with MC, sl 2 as if to k2tog, k1, pass 2 sl sts over; with CC, k5, p1, k2, sl 1 wyib, [k7, p1, k2, sl 1 wyib] 4 (4, 5, 5, 5) [6, 6, 6, 7, 7, 7] {8, 8, 8, 9, 9, 9} times, sm, knit to last 3 sts, m1, p1, k1e, sl 1 wyib. 2 sts inc'd and 2 sts dec'd; no change to st count.

Row 20 (WS): With CC, p1, sl 1 wyif, k1, purl to m, remove m, [BO 5 sts, p6] 4 (4, 5, 5, 5) [6, 6, 6, 7, 7, 7] {8, 8, 8, 9, 9, 9} times, BO 5, p3; with MC, k1; with CC, p3, BO 5 sts, [p6, BO 5 sts] 4 (4, 5, 5, 5) [6, 6, 6, 7, 7, 7] {8, 8, 8, 9, 9, 9} times, remove m, purl to last 3 sts, k1, sl 1 wyif, p1.

Cut yarns.
85 (89, 93, 95, 99, 103) [107, 111, 115, 119, 123, 125] {129, 133, 137, 141, 145, 149} sts rem.

Row 21 (RS): Join MC, sl 1 wyib, k1e, p1, knit to last 3 sts, p1, k1e, sl 1 wyib.

Row 22 (WS): P1, sl 1 wyif, k1, p39 (41, 43, 44, 46, 48) [50, 52, 54, 56, 58, 59] {61, 63, 65, 67, 69, 71}, place these 42 (44, 46, 47, 49, 51) [53, 55, 57, 59, 61, 62] {64, 66, 68, 70, 72, 74} sts on a holder for right shoulder, BO 1 st (center st, base of V-neck), k1, p3, w&t.

42 (44, 46, 47, 49, 51) [53, 55, 57, 59, 61, 62] {64, 66, 68, 70, 72, 74} sts rem on needle for left shoulder.

Left Shoulder short rows:
Row 1 (RS): K1, k2tog, p1, k1e, sl 1 wyib. 1 st dec'd at neck edge.

Row 2: P1, sl 1 wyif, k1, purl to previous wrapped st, purl wrap tog with st, p2, w&t.
Row 3: Knit to last 5 sts, k2tog, p1, k1e, sl 1 wyib. 1 st dec'd at neck edge.
Rep Rows 2–3 9 (10, 11, 11, 12, 12) [13, 14, 14, 15, 16, 16] {17, 17, 18, 19, 19, 20} more times. 31 (32, 33, 34, 35, 37) [38, 39, 41, 42, 43, 44] {45, 47, 48, 49, 51, 52} sts rem.

Next row (WS): P1, sl 1 wyif, k1, purl to previous wrapped st, purl wrap tog with st, purl to last 3 sts, k1, sl 1 wyif, p1.

Next row (RS): Sl 1 wyib, k1e, p1, knit to last 5 sts, k2tog, p1, k1e, sl 1 wyib. 1 st dec'd at neck edge.
Next row (WS): P1, sl 1 wyif, k1, purl to last 3 sts, k1, sl 1 wyif, p1.
Rep the last 2 rows 13 (14, 13, 14, 13, 15) [14, 15, 15, 16, 15, 16] {15, 17, 16, 17, 17, 18} more times. 17 (17, 19, 19, 21, 21) [23, 23, 25, 25, 27, 27] {29, 29, 31, 31, 33, 33} sts rem.

Work even, maintaining 3-st selvages at each end, until armhole measures 7.5 (7.75, 7.75, 8, 8, 8.5) [8.5, 9, 9, 9.5, 9.5, 9.75] {9.75, 10.25, 10.25, 10.75, 10.75, 11.25}" / 19 (19.5, 19.5, 20.5, 20.5, 21.5) [21.5, 23, 23, 24, 24, 25] {25, 26, 26, 27.5, 27.5, 28.5}cm, ending with a RS row. Place sts on holder.

Right Shoulder short rows:
Replace 42 (44, 46, 47, 49, 51) [53, 55, 57, 59, 61, 62] {64, 66, 68, 70, 72, 74} held sts on needle and join MC with RS facing.

Row 1 (RS): Sl 1 wyib, k1e, p1, ssk, k1, w&t. 1 st dec'd at neck edge.
Row 2 (WS): Purl to last 3 sts, k1, sl 1 wyif, p1.

Row 3: Sl 1 wyib, k1e, p1, ssk, knit to previous wrapped st, knit wrap tog with st, k2, w&t. 1 st dec'd at neck edge.
Row 4: Purl to last 3 sts, k1, sl 1 wyif, p1.
Rep Rows 3–4 9 (10, 11, 11, 12, 12) [13, 14, 14, 15, 16, 16] {17, 17, 18, 19, 19, 20} more times. 31 (32, 33, 34, 35, 37) [38, 39, 41, 42, 43, 44] {45, 47, 48, 49, 51, 52} sts rem.

Next row (RS): Sl 1 wyib, k1e, p1, ssk, knit to previous wrapped st, knit wrap tog with st, knit to last 3 sts, p1, k1e, sl 1 wyib. 1 st dec'd at neck edge.

Next row: P1, sl 1 wyif, k1, purl to last 3 sts, k1, sl 1 wyif, p1.
Next row: Sl 1 wyib, k1e, p1, ssk, knit to last 3 sts, p1, k1e, sl 1 wyib. 1 st dec'd at neck edge.
Rep the last 2 rows 13 (14, 13, 14, 13, 15) [14, 15, 15, 16, 15, 16] {15, 17, 16, 17, 17, 18} more times. 17 (17, 19, 19, 21, 21) [23, 23, 25, 25, 27, 27] {29, 29, 31, 31, 33, 33} sts rem.

Work even, maintaining 3-st selvages at each end, until armhole measures 7.5 (7.75, 7.75, 8, 8, 8.5) [8.5, 9, 9, 9.5, 9.5, 9.75] {9.75, 10.25, 10.25, 10.75, 10.75, 11.25}" / 19 (19.5, 19.5, 20.5, 20.5, 21.5) [21.5, 23, 23, 24, 24, 25] {25, 26, 26, 27.5, 27.5, 28.5}cm, ending with a RS row. Place sts on holder.

BACK

Read ahead! Armhole shaping, stockinette inset triangle, and neck shaping are worked simultaneously.

Replace 107 (113, 121, 127, 135, 141) [147, 155, 161, 167, 175, 181] {185, 195, 201, 209, 215, 221} held back sts on needle. Join yarn with WS facing.

Shape armholes:
Row 1 (WS): P1, sl 1 wyif, k1, work 51 (54, 58, 61, 65, 68) [71, 75, 78, 81, 85, 88] {90, 95, 98, 102, 105, 108} sts in patt, pm, work in patt to last 3 sts, k1, sl 1 wyif, p1.

Row 2 (RS): Sl 1 wyib, k1e, p1, [ssk] twice, work in patt to last 7 sts, [k2tog] 2 times, p1, k1e, sl 1 wyib. 4 sts dec'd.
Row 3: P1, sl 1 wyif, k1, work in patt to last 3 sts, k1, sl 1 wyif, p1.
Rep the last 2 rows 2 (2, 3, 4, 6, 6) [6, 8, 8, 8, 10, 11] {10, 12, 12, 14, 14, 14} more times.

2.25 (2.25, 2.5, 2.5, 2.75, 2.75)
[3, 3, 3.25, 3.25, 3.5, 3.5]
{3.75, 3.75, 4.25, 4.25, 4.5, 4.5}"

5.5 (5.5, 6.5, 6.5, 7, 7)
[7.5, 7.5, 8.5, 8.5, 9, 9]
{9.5, 9.5, 10.5, 10.5, 11, 11}cm

8.75 (8.75, 9, 9, 9.25, 9.25)
[9.5, 9.5, 9.75, 9.75, 10, 10]
{10.25, 10.25, 10.5, 10.5, 10.75, 10.75}"

21.5 (21.5, 22.5, 22.5, 23, 23)
[23.5, 23.5, 24.5, 24.5, 25]
{25.5, 25.5, 26.5, 26.5, 27, 27}cm

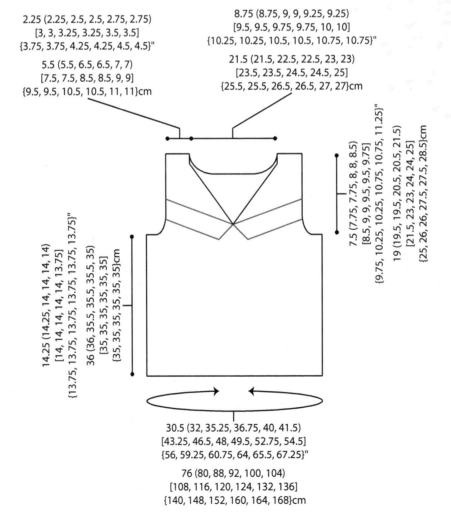

14.25 (14.25, 14, 14, 14, 14)
[14, 14, 14, 14, 14, 13.75]
{13.75, 13.75, 13.75, 13.75, 13.75, 13.75}"

36 (36, 35.5, 35.5, 35.5, 35)
[35, 35, 35, 35, 35, 35]
{35, 35, 35, 35, 35, 35}cm

7.5 (7.75, 7.75, 8, 8, 8.5)
[8.5, 9, 9, 9.5, 9.5, 9.75]
{9.75, 10.25, 10.25, 10.75, 10.75, 11.25}"

19 (19.5, 19.5, 20.5, 20.5, 21.5)
[21.5, 23, 23, 24, 24, 25]
{25, 26, 26, 27.5, 27.5, 28.5}cm

30.5 (32, 35.25, 36.75, 40, 41.5)
[43.25, 46.5, 48, 49.5, 52.75, 54.5]
{56, 59.25, 60.75, 64, 65.5, 67.25}"

76 (80, 88, 92, 100, 104)
[108, 116, 120, 124, 132, 136]
{140, 148, 152, 160, 164, 168}cm

Next row (RS): Sl 1 wyib, k1e, p1, ssk, work in patt to last 5 sts, k2tog, p1, k1e, sl 1 wyib. 2 sts dec'd.
Next row (WS): P1, sl 1 wyif, k1, work in patt to last 3 sts, k1, sl 1 wyif, p1.
Rep the last 2 rows 1 (2, 2, 2, 0, 1) [2, 0, 1, 2, 0, 0] {2, 1, 2, 0, 1, 2} more time(s).

91 (95, 99, 101, 105, 109) [113, 117, 121, 125, 129] {131, 135, 139, 143, 147, 151, 155} sts rem.

At the same time, when armhole measures approx. 1–1.5" / 2.5–4cm, ending with Row 2 (6, 6, 2, 2, 6) [2, 2, 6, 2, 2, 6] {2, 2, 6, 6, 2, 6} of lace patt, shape stockinette inset triangle:

Row 1 (RS): Work in patt to 1 st before m (ending with a yo), pm, k3 removing m, pm, work in patt (beg with a yo) to end.

Row 2 (WS): Work in patt to m, sm, purl to m, sm, work in patt to end.
Row 3 (RS): Work in patt to 2 sts before m (ending with a yo), pm, k2, remove m, knit to next m, remove m, k2, pm, work in patt (beg with a yo) to end.
Row 4: Rep Row 2.
Row 5: Work in patt to 1 st before m (ending with a yo), pm, k1, remove m, knit to next m, remove m, k1, pm, work in patt (beg with a yo) to end.
Work as set by Rows 2–5 until all lace sts have been incorporated into St st. Remove m and continue in St st with 3-st selvages.

At the same time, when armholes measure 1.75" / 4.5cm less than front to shoulder, ending with a WS row, shape neck:

Next row (RS): Work 33 (33, 35, 35, 37, 37) [39, 39, 41, 41, 43, 43] {45, 45, 47, 47, 49, 49} sts in patt, join a second ball of yarn and BO 25 (29, 29, 31, 31, 35) [35, 39, 39, 43, 43, 45] {45, 49, 49, 53, 53, 57} sts, work in patt to end.

Working both shoulders at the same time with separate balls of yarn:
Next row (WS): On left shoulder, p1, sl 1 wyif, k1, work to last 3 sts, k1, sl 1 wyif, k1; work right shoulder the same.

Next row (RS): On right shoulder, work to last 8 sts, k2tog, k3tog, work to end; on left shoulder, work 3 sts, sssk, ssk, work to end. 3 sts dec'd each side of neck.
Work 1 WS row even.
Rep the last 2 rows 2 more times.

Next row (RS): On right shoulder, work to last 6 sts, k3tog, work to end; on left shoulder, work 3 sts, sssk, work to end. 2 sts dec'd each side of neck.
Work 1 WS row even.
Rep the last 2 rows once more.

Next row (RS): On right shoulder, work to last 5 sts, k2tog, work to end; on left shoulder, work 3 sts, ssk, work to end. 1 st dec'd each side of neck.
Work 1 WS row even.
Rep the last 2 rows 2 more times.

17 (17, 19, 19, 21, 21) [23, 23, 25, 25, 27, 27] {29, 29, 31, 31, 33, 33} sts rem each shoulder.

FINISHING

Graft shoulders together using Kitchener stitch.
Weave in ends.

Shape pleats by folding on the slipped st and purled columns, each gill section folded toward the center front. (In paper-folding terms, the slipped st columns are "mountains" and the purl columns are "valleys"). Sew in place by whip stitching the BO and CO sts down.

Block to dimensions shown in schematic.

NUCLEAR WINTER

Baby, it's cold outside ... and it's likely to stay that way for at least a few years. So start bundling up and hoarding firewood! Oh, and watch out for mutants.

Situation: Repeated nuclear attacks have plunged the Earth into shadow, blocking the sun with vast clouds of dust and debris. Or perhaps a super-volcano has erupted, or an asteroid has smashed into Earth—same idea. Until that dust settles, it's going to be mighty chilly.

FISSION

Annika Barranti

In the cold days ahead, keep your hands cozy while maintaining much needed dexterity with a pair of these stylish mitts. Like murderous atoms on a bender, the cables on these mitts join and split, weaving around, making and breaking bonds as they please, and never letting you forget just what got you here in the first place.

PATTERN NOTES

These mitts are worked from the top (fingers) down, which allows the knitter to easily customize the length to preference or available yarn. The i-cord ties are worked last, and could be omitted for a more streamlined mitt (or to conserve yarn).

Choose a worsted-weight yarn with good stitch definition. You will be working twisted stitches and cables at a tighter-than-recommended gauge for a sturdy fabric.

It is strongly advised to divide your yarn in half before you begin, and to work the thumb first; this way you eliminate guesswork and minimize ends to weave in, as you will not have to cut your yarn to work the thumb.

Note: Wrist repeat should be worked 11 (13) times total.

During the thumb gusset, some rnds will have 2 knit or 2 purl sts adjacent to each other; this will be corrected on subsequent decrease rnds.

PATTERN: LEFT MITT

THUMB

CO 14 (16) sts and join to work in the round.

[K1 tbl, p1] to end for 10 (12) rnds. Transfer sts to holder or waste yarn and set aside.

UPPER HAND

CO 44 (52) sts and join to work in the round. 17 (21) palm sts, 27 (31) back of hand sts.

Rnd 1: P1, [k1 tbl, p1] 8 (10) times, work Rnd 1 of the Left Chart.

Rnds 2–21 (2–27): P1, [k1 tbl, p1] 8 (10) times, work next rnd of Left Chart.

Attach thumb:

Rnd 22 (28): Sl 4 sts to waste yarn, work across 10 (12) thumb sts, leaving last 4 thumb sts on waste yarn, pm, work 13 (17) sts as est, work next rnd of Left Chart. 50 (60) sts.

CUFF

Rnds 23–24 (29–30): Work sts as est, working next rnd of Left Chart.
Rnd 25 (31): P2tog tbl, [k1 tbl, p1] 3 (4) times, k2tog tbl, sm, p1, [k1 tbl, p1] 6 (8) times, work next rnd of Left Chart. 48 (58) sts.

Rnds 26–27 (32–33): Work as est, working the next rnd of Left Chart.
Rnd 28 (34): Ssk, [p1, k1 tbl] 2 (3) times, ssk, sm, p1, [k1 tbl, p1] 6 (8) times, work next rnd of Left Chart. 46 (56) sts.

Rnds 29–30 (35–36): Work all sts as est.

SIZES

S (L); shown in size S

Sized to fit hand circumference of up to 7.5 (9)" / 19 (23)cm

FINISHED MEASUREMENTS

Length: 10 (12)" / 25.5 (30.5)cm
Palm Circumference: 6 (7)" / 15 (18)cm unstretched

MATERIALS

Lorna's Laces Shepherd Worsted (100% superwash merino; 225 yds / 206m per 100g skein); color: Pewter; 1 (2) skeins

Set of US #5 / 3.75mm dpns, or size needed to obtain gauge

Cable needle, stitch markers, stitch holders or waste yarn, yarn needle

GAUGE

32 sts and 31 rounds = 4" / 10 cm in [k1 tbl, p1] rib, unstretched

As the twisted rib allows a great deal of stretch, row gauge is slightly more important than stitch gauge. If you cannot achieve row gauge, you may need to work more or fewer cable pattern repeats (or more plain rows between cables) to achieve the correct length.

Rnd 31 (37): P2tog, [k1 tbl, p1] 1 (2) times, k2tog tbl, remove m, p1, [k1 tbl, p1] 6 (8) times, work next rnd of Left Chart. 44 (54) sts.

Rnds 32–78 (38–94): P1, [k1 tbl, p1] 8 (11) times, work next rnd of Left Chart.

WORK BO AND TIES

Palm stitches: P1, k1 tbl, insert left needle through both loops and knit together, [work next st as presented, insert left needle through both loops and knit together], rep across until 16 (21) sts have been bound off. Sl 1 rem st from right needle to dpn.

Outer hand sts: K2 to dpn. Work 3-st i-cord for 10" / 25.5cm or to desired length. BO and cut yarn. Attach yarn and knit next 3 sts to dpn. Work 3-st i-cord for 10" / 25.5cm or to desired length. BO and cut yarn.

Attach yarn to rem live sts and BO 16 (21) sts as for palm sts. Sl 1 rem st from right needle to dpn, k2. Work 3-st i-cord for 10" / 25.5cm or to desired length. BO and cut yarn. Attach yarn and knit next 3 sts to dpn. Work 3-st i-cord for 10" / 25.5cm or to desired length. BO and cut yarn.

PATTERN: RIGHT MITT

THUMB

CO 14 (16) sts and join to work in the round.

[P1, k1 tbl] to end for 10 (12) rnds. Transfer sts to holder or waste yarn and set aside.

UPPER HAND

CO 44 (52) sts and join to work in the round. 27 (31) back of hand sts, 17 (21) palm sts.

Rnd 1: Work Rnd 1 of Right Chart over 27 (31) sts, p1, [k1 tbl, p1] 8 (10) times.

Rnds 2–21 (2–27): Work next rnd of Right Chart, p1, [k1 tbl, p1] 8 (10) times.

Attach thumb:

Rnd 22 (28): Work next rnd of Right Chart, p1, [k1 tbl, p1] 6 (8) times, pm, sl 4 sts to waste yarn, sl 4 thumb sts to waste yarn, work across 10 (12) thumb sts. 50 (60) sts.

CUFF

Rnds 23–24 (29–30): Work as est. Rnd 25 (31): Work next rnd of Right Chart, p1, [k1 tbl, p1] 6 (8) times, sm, k2tog tbl, [k1 tbl, p1] 3 (4) times, p2tog tbl. 48 (58) sts.

Rnds 26–27 (32–33): Work as est. Rnd 28 (34): Work next rnd of Right Chart, p1, [k1 tbl, p1] 6 (8) times, sm, ssk, [p1, k1 tbl] 2 (3) times, ssk. 46 (56) sts.

Rnds 29–30 (35–36): Work as est.

Rnd 31 (37): Work next rnd of Right Chart, p1, [k1 tbl, p1] 6 (8) times, remove m, k2tog, [p1, k1 tbl] 1 (2) times, p2tog tbl. 44 (54) sts.

Rnds 32–78 (38–94): Work next rnd of Right Chart, p1, [k1 tbl, p1] 8 (11) times.

WORK BO AND TIES

K3 to dpn. Work 3-st i-cord for 10" / 25.5cm or to desired length. BO and cut yarn. Attach yarn and knit next 3 sts to dpn. Work 3-st i-cord for 10" / 25.5cm or to desired length. BO and cut yarn. Attach yarn and BO 16 (21) sts as follows: p1, k1 tbl, insert left needle through both loops and knit together, [work next st as presented, insert left needle through both loops and knit together]. K3 to dpn. Work 3-st i-cord for 10" / 25.5cm or to desired length. BO and cut yarn. K3 to dpn. Work 3-st i-cord for 10" / 25.5cm or to desired length. BO and cut yarn. Attach yarn and knit next 3 sts to dpn. Work 3-st i-cord for 10" / 25.5cm or to desired length. BO and cut yarn. Attach yarn and BO 16 (21) sts as before.

FINISHING

Graft sts at thumb join. Weave in ends. Tie i-cords as desired. To block, stretch gloves vertically (wrist to fingers) to straighten columns of sts. No wet blocking required!

LEFT MITT SIZE S

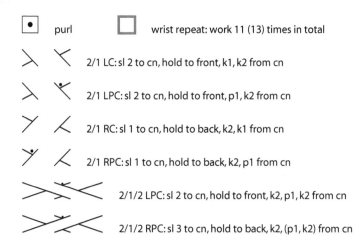

	purl		wrist repeat: work 11 (13) times in total

2/1 LC: sl 2 to cn, hold to front, k1, k2 from cn

2/1 LPC: sl 2 to cn, hold to front, p1, k2 from cn

2/1 RC: sl 1 to cn, hold to back, k2, k1 from cn

2/1 RPC: sl 1 to cn, hold to back, k2, p1 from cn

2/1/2 LPC: sl 2 to cn, hold to front, k2, p1, k2 from cn

2/1/2 RPC: sl 3 to cn, hold to back, k2, (p1, k2) from cn

RIGHT MITT SIZE S

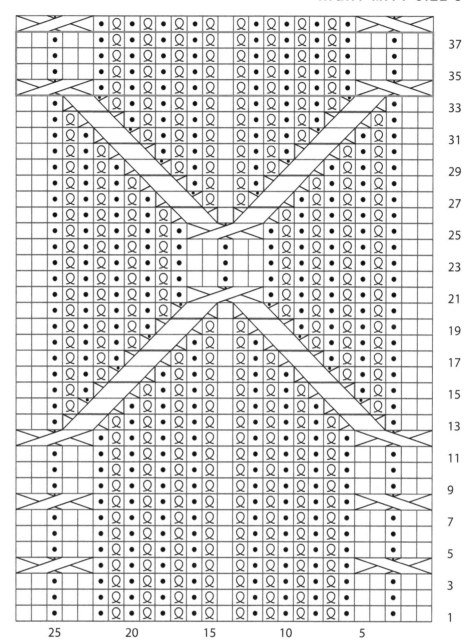

37

35

33

31

29

27

25

23

21

19

17

15

13

11

9

7

5

3

1

25   20   15   10   5

LEFT MITT SIZE L

RIGHT MITT SIZE L

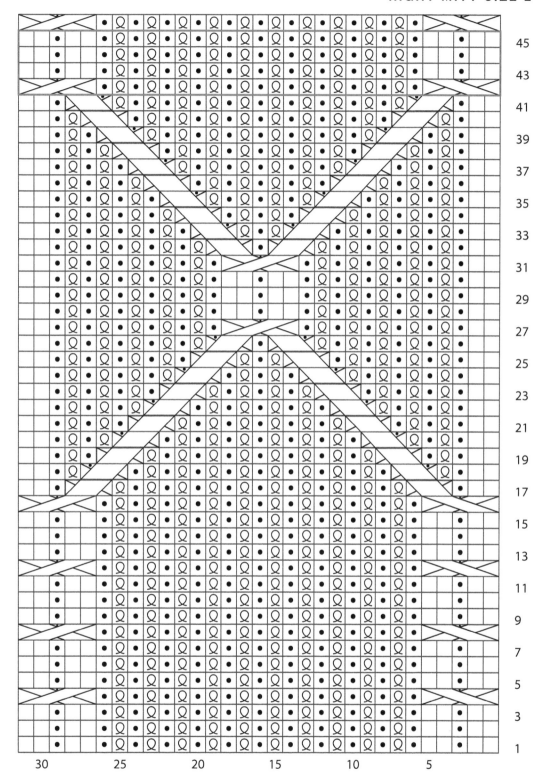

45
43
41
39
37
35
33
31
29
27
25
23
21
19
17
15
13
11
9
7
5
3
1

30 25 20 15 10 5

I WAS A TEENAGE MUTANT

Alexandra Tinsley

Now, if there's one thing all those comics and cartoons have taught us about mutating, it's that it's really anybody's guess what you're going to get. Super awesome psychic powers? Very possibly. Extra limbs and general blobbiness? Also pretty likely. Luckily for this hat, its mutations are pretty benign and mostly take the form of an unusual crown structure.

PATTERN NOTES

This hat is knit in the round with no shaping. The crown is closed by dividing the stitches into four sections, and grafting each section together with the section directly across from it: first one set, and then the other, over the top of the first.

PATTERN

With circular needle, CO 90 sts. Pm and join to work in the round. Work in garter st (knit 1 rnd, purl 1 rnd) for 28 rnds. Knit every rnd until piece measures 8" / 20.5cm from CO.

CLOSE CROWN

Put next 12 sts on holder, then the next 20 sts on a dpn. Put the next 25 sts on waste yarn or holder, then the next 20 on another dpn. Put the last 13 sts on the waste yarn or holder that has the initial 12 sts.

Using Kitchener stitch, graft the two sets of 20 sts on the dpns together.

Place the two section of 25 stitches that are on holders onto two dpns, and then graft these sts together, bridging them over top of the first grafted seam.

FINISHING

Weave in all ends and block gently.

SIZE

One size

FINISHED MEASUREMENTS

Circumference: 18.5" / 46cm, unstretched
Height: 8" / 20.5cm

MATERIALS

Dream in Color Classy with Cashmere (70% superwash merino, 20% cashmere, 10% nylon; 210 yds / 192m per 113g skein); color: Scorched Lime; 1 skein

16-inch US #7 / 4.5mm circular needle, or size needed to obtain gauge

Two US #7 / 4.5mm dpns to use while grafting top

Stitch marker, stitch holders or waste yarn, yarn needle

GAUGE

19.5 sts and 30 rounds = 4" / 10 cm in St st

FALLOUT

Alexandra Tinsley

"Watch out where the fallout goes, and don't you eat that dirty snow..." —Frank Zapocalypse

A warm woolen layer to keep ears cozy, a touch of glitter to keep spirits up, and a bit of a camo-snow-effect to help you blend in. So what if that metal tinsel is almost definitely "hot"? (And I don't mean sexy.)

PATTERN NOTES

This hood is constructed first by working a flared garter stitch cowl using short rows, and then picking up stitches from the top edge and knitting the hood upwards, finishing by joining in the round and decreasing at the crown.

PATTERN

Using a provisional method and circular needle, CO 4 sts, pm, CO 4 sts, pm, CO 12 sts. 20 sts. Do not join.
Row 1 and all odd-numbered rows: Knit.
Row 2: Knit to first m, sm, w&t.
Row 4: Knit to end, picking up the wrap as you come to it and knitting it together with the wrapped stitch.
Row 6: Knit to second m, sm, w&t.
Row 8: Knit to end, picking up the wrap as you come to it and working it together with the wrapped stitch.

Rep these 8 rows until shorter edge of piece measures 16" / 40.5cm from CO. Remove waste yarn from provisional CO and place these 20 sts on spare needle. Join the live sts to the CO sts using a 3-needle BO. Turn work so seam is on inside.

Beginning in the center front of the cowl (opposite the seam), pick up and knit 54 sts (approx. 3 sts per 4 rows) around the cowl. Do not join. Turn work.

Row 1 (WS): Sl 2 wyif, purl to end.
Row 2 (RS): Sl 2 wyib, knit to end.
Rep these 2 rows until piece measures 9" / 23 cm from pick-up row, ending with Row 1.

Next row (RS): Sl 2 wyib, m1, knit to last 2 sts, m1, k2, pm and join to work in the rnd. 56 sts.
Knit 2 rnds.

SHAPE CROWN

Change to dpns when necessary.
Rnd 1: [K5, k2tog] to end. 48 sts.
Rnds 2, 4, 6, 8: Knit.
Rnd 3: [K4, k2tog] to end. 40 sts.
Rnd 5: [K3, k2tog] to end. 32 sts.
Rnd 7: [K2, k2tog] to end. 24 sts.
Rnd 9: [K1, k2tog] to end. 16 sts.
Rnd 10: [K2tog] to end. 8 sts.

FINISHING

Cut yarn and draw tail through rem sts. Pull snug. Weave in all ends and block gently.

SIZE

One size

FINISHED MEASUREMENTS

Neck: 16" / 40.5cm unstretched at narrowest point, 30" / 76cm at widest

Height: Approx. 17" / 43cm from bottom of cowl to top of hood

Hood: Approx. 9" / 23cm deep

MATERIALS

Knit Collage Pixie Dust Mini (98% wool, 1% angelina, 1% mohair; 80 yds / 73m per 100g skein); color: Crystal Avalanche; 2 skeins

16-inch US #11 / 8mm circular needle, or size needed to obtain gauge
Set of US #11 / 8mm dpns
Spare US #11 / 8mm needle for working 3-needle BO

Stitch markers, waste yarn for provisional CO, yarn needle

GAUGE

11 sts and 16 rows = 4" / 10 cm in St st
10 sts and 20 rows = 4" / 10 cm in garter st

Due to the nature of this yarn (a hand-spun single), the gauge can vary from one section of knitting to another. Parts of the work may be looser or tighter; aim for a fabric that averages out to the gauges above.

ALPACALYPSE

Michele Moskaluk

To make it through the harsh and enduring winter, survivors will obviously need warm clothes. Luckily, you are armed with knitting needles and chunky yarn made from the few mutant alpacas left roaming the earth. This jacket uses the honeycomb brioche stitch to create an extra thick, yet flexible, body. The sleeves are ribbed and close-fitting but stretchy enough to provide with the range of motion you need when protecting your turf, hunting alpacas, and making toxic snowmen. Plus, it's very snuggly. The world may have ended but sweaters can still be comfy! Just watch out for those mutant alpacas, they pack a nasty bite.

STITCHES AND TECHNIQUES

HONEYCOMB BRIOCHE ST

(Multiple of 2 sts) Note: Do not count yarn overs as stitches.
Set-up Row 1 (WS): [K1, yo, sl 1 pwise wyib] to end.
Set-up Row 2 (RS): K1, [sl the yo pwise wyib, k2] to last st, sl the yo pwise, k1.
Pattern Row 1 (WS): [Yo, sl 1 pwise wyib, knit the next st and yo tog] to end.
Pattern Row 2 (RS): [K2, sl the yo pwise wyib] to end.
Pattern Row 3: [Knit the next st and yo tog, yo, sl 1 pwise wyib] to end.
Pattern Row 4: K1, [sl the yo pwise wyib, k2] to last st, sl the yo pwise, k1.
Rep Pattern Rows 1–4.

PATTERN NOTES

The body is made flat in one piece from the bottom up to the armholes, then divided and fronts and back are worked separately to the shoulder. Sleeves are made in the round from the bottom up to the cap and then finished flat. After shoulder seams are joined, stitches are picked up around the bottom and inner hems and neckline for the bands and collar.

When binding off in Honeycomb Brioche st, work in patt as written, except do not make any new yarn overs. For instance, if you're binding off stitches on Pattern Row 3, work [knit the next st and yo together, sl 1 pwise wyib].

PATTERN

BODY

With larger needle and MC, CO 56 (64, 72, 80, 84, 92, 100) sts. Work Honeycomb Brioche Set-up Rows 1 and 2. Rep Pattern Rows 1–4 of Honeycomb Brioche until piece measures 14.5 (14.5, 15.5, 15.5, 16, 16.5, 17)" / 37 (37, 39.5, 39.5, 40.5, 42, 43)cm, ending with a WS row.

Divide for armholes (RS): Work 12 (14, 16, 18, 19, 20, 22) sts in patt and place on holder for right front, BO 3 (3, 3, 3, 3, 5, 5) sts, work in patt until there are 26 (30, 34, 38, 40, 42, 46) sts on right needle and place on holder for back,

SIZES

Women's XS (S, M, L, XL, 2X, 3X); shown in size S

Intended to be worn with 3–4" / 7.5–10cm of positive ease

FINISHED MEASUREMENTS

Bust: 33.5 (38, 42.75, 47.25, 49.5, 54, 58.75)" / 83.5 (95, 106.5, 118, 123.5, 135, 146.5)cm

MATERIALS

[MC] Blue Sky Alpacas Bulky (50% alpaca, 50% wool; 44 yds / 41m per 100g skein); color: Dark Grey 1007; 5 (6, 7, 8, 9, 10, 11) skeins

[CC] Blue Sky Alpacas Worsted Hand Dyes (50% merino, 50% alpaca; 100 yds / 91m per 100g skein); color: White 2003; 4 (4, 4, 5, 5, 5, 6) skeins

40-inch US #15 / 10mm circular needle, or size needed to obtain gauge
40-inch US #10 / 6mm circular needle, or size needed to obtain gauge
US #10 / 6mm dpns

Stitch markers, removable markers, six 1.5" / 38mm toggle buttons, stitch holders, yarn needle

GAUGE

7 sts and 20 rows = 4" / 10cm in Honeycomb Brioche st with MC on larger needle

Note that 20 rows in Brioche st looks like 10 rows, because there are slipped sts on every row.

18 sts and 21 rows = 4" / 10cm in [k2, p2] rib with CC on smaller needle

BO 3 (3, 3, 3, 5, 5) sts, work to end. 12 (14, 16, 18, 19, 20, 22) sts rem for left front.

LEFT FRONT

Work 1 WS row even.
BO 1 (2, 3, 3, 3, 3, 4) sts at beg of next row (RS), then BO 1 (2, 2, 3, 3, 3, 3) sts at beg of foll RS row. 10 (10, 11, 12, 13, 14, 15) sts.

Work even until armhole measures 6.25 (6.75, 7.25, 7.5, 8, 8.5)" / 16 (17, 18.5, 19, 20.5, 21.5)cm, ending with a RS row.

Shape neck and shoulder:
BO 2 (2, 3, 3, 3, 3, 3) sts at beg of next row (WS), then BO 1 st at beg of next 1 (1, 1, 1, 2, 2, 2) WS row(s). 7 (7, 7, 8, 8, 9, 10) sts.

Next row (RS): BO 2 (2, 2, 3, 3, 3, 4) sts, work to end.
Work 1 WS row even.
BO rem 5 (5, 5, 5, 5, 6, 6) sts.

RIGHT FRONT

Return 12 (14, 16, 18, 19, 20, 22) held sts to needle and join yarn with WS facing.
BO 1 (2, 3, 3, 3, 3, 4) sts at beg of next row (WS), then BO 1 (2, 2, 3, 3, 3, 3) sts at beg of foll WS row. 10 (10, 11, 12, 13, 14, 15) sts.
Work even until armhole measures 6.25 (6.75, 7.25, 7.5, 8, 8.5)" / 16 (17, 18.5, 19, 20.5, 21.5)cm, ending with a WS row.

Shape neck and shoulder:
BO 2 (2, 3, 3, 3, 3, 3) sts at beg of next row (RS), then BO 1 st at beg of next 1 (1, 1, 1, 2, 2, 2) RS row(s). 7 (7, 7, 8, 8, 9, 10) sts.

Next row (WS): BO 2 (2, 2, 3, 3, 3, 4) sts, work to end.
Work 1 RS row even.
BO rem 5 (5, 5, 5, 5, 6, 6) sts.

BACK

Return 26 (30, 34, 38, 40, 42, 46) held sts to needle and join yarn with WS facing.

BO 1 (2, 3, 3, 3, 3, 4) sts at beg of next 2 rows, then BO 1 (2, 2, 3, 3, 3, 3) sts at beg of foll 2 rows. 22 (22, 24, 26, 28, 30, 32) sts.

Work even until armholes measure 6.75 (7.25, 7.75, 8.25, 8.5, 9, 9.5)" / 17 (18.5, 19.5, 21, 21.5, 23, 24)cm.
BO 2 (2, 2, 3, 3, 3, 4) sts at beg of next 2 rows.
BO rem 18 (18, 20, 20, 22, 24, 24) sts.

SLEEVES

Using CC and dpns, CO 28 (28, 32, 32, 36, 40, 40) sts. Pm and join to work in the round.
Rnd 1: K1, [p2, k2] to last 3 sts, p2, k1.
Rep last rnd 5 more times.

Inc Rnd: K1, m1, work to last st, m1, k1. 2 sts inc'd.
Working inc'd sts into rib, rep Inc Rnd on every 8th (6th, 6th, 5th, 4th, 4th, 3rd) rnd 11 (13, 14, 17, 20, 21, 25) more times. 52 (56, 62, 68, 78, 84, 92) sts.
Work even until sleeve measures 19" / 48.5cm.

Shape cap:
BO 5 (5, 5, 5, 5, 6, 6) sts, work to end. Turn and begin working back and forth.

Next row (WS): BO 5 (5, 5, 5, 5, 6, 6) sts, work to end. 42 (46, 52, 58, 68, 70, 78) sts.
BO 1 st at beg of next 8 (10, 28, 32, 26, 28, 26) rows. 34 (36, 24, 26, 42, 44, 54) sts.

Sizes XS (S) only:
Work 2 rows even.
BO 1 st at beg of next 10 (12) rows. 24 (24) sts.

All sizes:
BO 2 sts at beg of next 2 (2, 2, 2, 6, 6, 4) rows. 20 (20, 20, 22, 30, 32, 46) sts.
BO 3 sts at beg of next 2 (2, 2, 2, 4, 4, 8) rows.
BO rem 14 (14, 14, 16, 18, 20, 22) sts.

Sew shoulder seams. Set sleeves into armholes.

Bottom ribbing:
Using CC and smaller needle, with RS facing, pick up and knit 158 (182, 206, 230, 242, 262, 286) sts from CO edge of body.

Row 1 (WS): [K2, p2] to last 2 sts, k2.
Row 2 (RS): [P2, k2] to last 2 sts, p2.
Rep Rows 1–2 four more times, then Row 1 once more.
BO loosely in rib.

Bands and collar:
Using CC and smaller needle, with RS facing and beg at right front bottom edge, pick up and knit 85 (89, 93, 93, 97, 101, 105) sts along right front edge to beg of neck shaping, pm, pick up and knit 40 (40, 48, 48, 56, 56, 60) sts around neckline, pm, pick up and knit 85 (89, 93, 93, 97, 101, 105) sts down left front edge. 210 (218, 234, 234, 250, 258, 270) sts.

Row 1 (WS): [P2, k2] to last 2 sts, p2.
Row 2 (RS): [Work in est rib to 1 st before m, m1L, k1, sm, k1, m1R] 2 times, work to end. 4 sts inc'd.

Row 3: Work in est rib, working inc'd sts into patt.
Row 4: Place removable markers for six buttonholes along the left front, evenly spaced, with the lowest button about 2" / 5cm from the bottom and the top button about 2" / 5cm from the base of the neck. [Work in est rib to 1 st before m, m1L, k1, sm, k1, m1R] 2 times, [work to m, BO 3 sts] 6 times, work to end.

Row 5: Work in est rib, CO 3 sts over each 3-st BO from previous row.
Row 6: Rep Row 2.
Row 7: Rep Row 3.
BO all sts in rib.

Weave in ends and block. Sew on buttons.

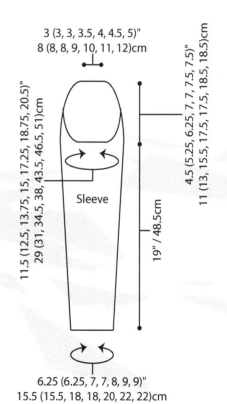

4 (4, 4, 4.5, 4.5, 5.25, 5.75)"
10 (10, 10, 11.5, 11.5, 13, 14.5)cm

4.5 (4.5, 5.75, 5.75, 6.75, 6.75, 6.75)"
11.5 (11.5, 14.5, 14.5, 17, 17, 17)cm

0.5" / 1.5cm

6.75 (7.25, 7.75, 8.25, 8.5, 9, 9.5)"
17 (18.5, 19.5, 21, 21.5, 23, 24)cm

Body

14.5 (14.5, 15.5, 15.5, 16, 16.5, 17)"
37 (37, 39.5, 39.5, 40.5, 42, 43)cm

32 (36.5, 41.25, 45.75, 48, 52.5, 57.25)"
80 (91.5, 103, 114.5, 120, 131.5, 143)cm

3 (3, 3, 3.5, 4, 4.5, 5)"
8 (8, 8, 9, 10, 11, 12)cm

4.5 (5.25, 6.25, 7, 7, 7.5, 7.5)"
11 (13, 15.5, 17.5, 17.5, 18.5, 18.5)cm

11.5 (12.5, 13.75, 15, 17.25, 18.75, 20.5)"
29 (31, 34.5, 38, 43.5, 46.5, 51)cm

Sleeve

19" / 48.5cm

6.25 (6.25, 7, 7, 8, 9, 9)"
15.5 (15.5, 18, 18, 20, 22, 22)cm

BABY'S FIRST PRINCIPLES

Amy Manning

Give your little one—and her descendants—a head start after the apocalypse with this baby blanket illustrating the most important principle of survival: avoid radiation. Even if the survivors forget what the radiation hazard symbol means, this blanket's motifs warn of its dangers. The center section is a large-scale all-over pattern depicting the radiation trefoil. The blanket is edged with two bands of motifs. The inner border is a small pattern of skulls, showing that the trefoil indicates danger. The outer border has running figures, illustrating the need to flee areas and objects labeled with the trefoil. Truly, the A-B-C's of the future.

PATTERN NOTES

This square blanket is knit in the round from the center out. Increases are placed both sides of the four corner stitches, every round. Knitting begins on double-pointed needles, then switches to progressively longer circular needles as needed.

STITCHES AND TECHNIQUES

Increases are worked as backward loops on either side of the four corner stitches, using the color called for in the chart. Twist the backward loops in opposite directions in order to keep the increases symmetrical around each corner stitch.

Each row of the charts is to be worked four times per round. The leftmost stitch of each chart is the marked corner stitch.

PATTERN

With MC and dpn, CO 8 sts (2 on each of 4 needles) and join to work in the round.

Work Rnd 1 of Setup Chart 4 times across the rnd, placing a locking marker on each corner st (the last st on each dpn). 12 sts.
Work Rnds 2–9 of Setup chart. 80 sts.

Work Rnds 1–18 of Diamond chart twice, then Rnds 1–9 once more, changing to progressively longer circular needles as needed. 440 sts.

Work Rnds 1–10 of Skull chart. 520 sts.
Work Rnds 1–12 of Edging chart. 616 sts.

Change to smaller needle and CC2.
Next rnd: [M1 backward loop, knit to marked st, m1 backward loop, knit marked st] 4 times. 8 sts inc'd.
Next rnd: [M1 backward loop, purl to marked st, m1 backward loop, purl marked st] 4 times. 8 sts inc'd.
Rep the last 2 rnds 4 more times. 696 sts.
BO all sts.

FINISHING

Weave in all ends. Wet block blanket, shaping as necessary and drying flat.

SIZE

One size

FINISHED MEASUREMENTS

36.5" / 91.5cm square

MATERIALS

Skacel HiKoo Simplicity (55% merino superwash, 28% acrylic, 17% nylon; 117 yds / 107m per 50g skein)

☢ [MC] Silver Hair #036; 4 skeins
☢ [CC1] Seattle Sky #038; 4 skeins
☢ [CC2] Gun Metal Grey #037; 3 skeins

Set of five US #5 / 3.75mm dpns, or size needed to obtain gauge
US #5 / 3.75 mm circular needles in the following lengths: 16-, 24-, 32-, 40-, and 48-inch

48-inch US #4 / 3.5mm circular needle

4 locking stitch markers, yarn needle

GAUGE

19 sts and 19 rounds = 4" / 10cm in stranded color patt, on larger needle

19 sts and 38 rnds = 4" / 10cm in garter stitch, on smaller needle

DIAMOND CHART

SETUP CHART

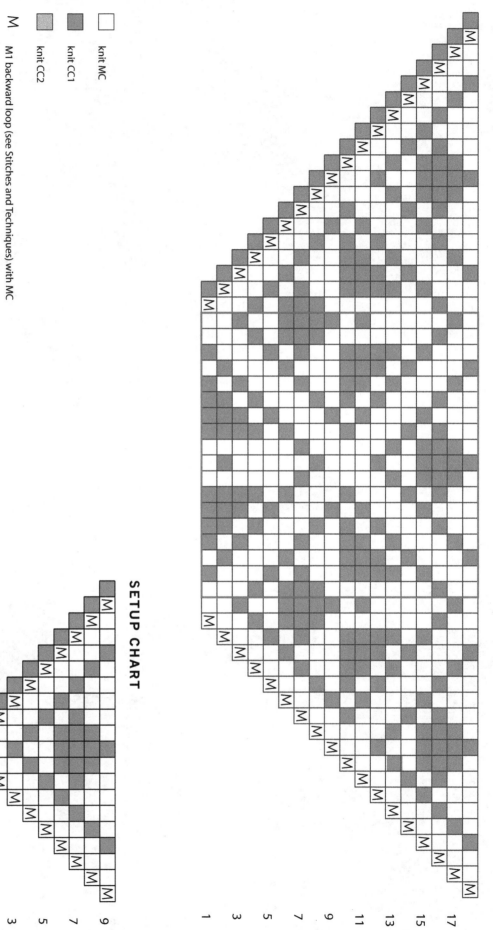

- ☐ knit MC
- ▨ knit CC1
- ▨ knit CC2
- M M1 backward loop (see Stitches and Techniques) with MC
- M M1 backward loop with CC1
- M M1 backward loop with CC2
- ◆ knit CC1 in first repeat only, otherwise knit MC
- ◇ knit CC1, except last repeat knit MC
- ☐ pattern repeat

SKULL CHART

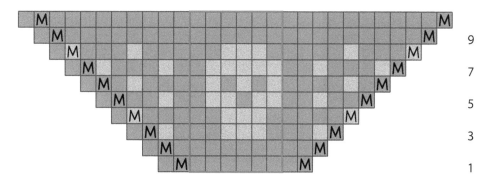

9

7

5

3

1

EDGING CHART

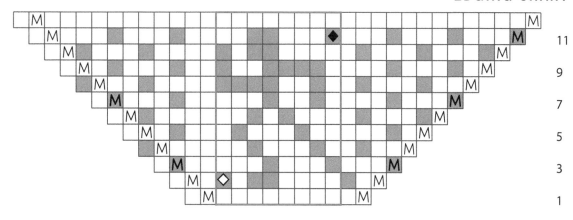

11

9

7

5

3

1

LONG ROAD AHEAD

Katherine Vaughan

It seems like one thing that post-apocalyptic fiction agrees on is that we'll be walking a lot after the end of civilization. With all that walking going on, you'll need a good set of boots as well as sturdy socks. For some reason, the books tend not to focus on socks…. These worsted-weight cuties are designed for heavy use. They have a slipped stitch pattern to cushion the feet and a short leg tailored for wear with ankle boots, and work up so quickly you'll be able to wear a pair and trade another for supplies!

PATTERN NOTES

These socks are worked from the top down, with a cushy slipped-stitch pattern that will be familiar to experienced sock knitters as one of the standard heel flap stitches. In this case the whole sock is worked in Eye of Partridge, resulting in a very cozy, warm garment. A gusset is started at the ankle to accommodate the extra width needed there, then short rows shape the shallow heel, and stitches are removed under the sole to create a reverse gusset that cups the heel. The toe is decreased slightly then grafted closed. Right and Left socks are worked to mirror each other because a slight seam will show; mirroring allows this seam to be located on the inside ankle.

STITCHES AND TECHNIQUES

M1 BACKWARD LOOP

Inc 1 st by making a backward loop over the right needle.

EYE OF PARTRIDGE STITCH

(Worked in the round, mult of 2 sts)
Rnd 1: [K1, sl 1 pwise wyib] to end.
Rnd 2: Knit.
Rnd 3: [Sl 1 pwise wyib, k1] to end.
Rnd 4: Knit.
Rep Rnds 1–4.

(Worked flat, mult of 2 sts)
Row 1 (RS): [K1, sl 1 pwise wyib] to end.
Row 2 (WS): Purl.
Row 3: [Sl 1 pwise wyib, k1] to end.
Row 4: Purl.
Rep Rows 1–4.

PATTERN: RIGHT SOCK

CUFF

CO 28 (32, 36, 40) sts, pm and join to work in the round.
Work in [k2, p2] rib for 4 rnds.
Inc Rnd: Work in rib, inc 4 sts evenly spaced. 32 (36, 40, 44) sts.

LEG

Work in Eye of Partridge Stitch until Leg measures 4 (4, 4.5, 5)" / 10 (10, 11.5, 12.5)cm from CO, ending with Rnd 4.
Note: This is the length to the ankle bone; for a longer sock, work more repeats of the Eye of Partridge Stitch.

Work Rnd 1 once more, placing a second marker for side after the 16th (18th, 20th, 22nd) stitch.

ANKLE GUSSET

Rnd 1: K1, m1 backward loop, knit to 1 st before m, m1 backward loop, k1, sm, knit to end. 2 sts inc'd.

SIZES

Women's S (M, L, XL); shown in size M

Sized to fit foot circumferences: 7 (8, 9, 10)" / 18 (20.5, 23, 25.5)cm

FINISHED MEASUREMENTS

Foot circumference: 6.75 (7.5, 8.5, 9.25)" / 17 (19, 21, 23)cm

Finished leg length: 5.25 (5.25, 5.75, 6.25)" / 13.5 (13.5, 14.5, 16)cm or adjustable to fit

Finished foot length: 8 (9, 10, 11)" / 20.5 (23, 25.5, 28)cm or adjustable to fit

MATERIALS

Skacel HiKoo Simpliworsted (55% merino superwash, 28% acrylic, 17% nylon; 140 yds / 128m per 100g skein); color: #038 Seattle Sky; 2 (2, 3, 3) skeins

Set of US #8 / 5mm dpns or circular needles for magic loop or 2-circulars techniques

3 removable stitch markers, yarn needle

GAUGE

19 sts and 26 rnds = 4" / 10 cm in Eye of Partridge st

16 sts and 24 rows = 4" / 10 cm in St st

Rnd 2: Work in patt as est, working a knit stitch into the m1 backward loop sts. Rep these 2 rnds 3 more times. 40 (44, 48, 52) sts.

Knit 1 rnd.

HEEL

Row 1 (RS): Work in patt to 1 st before end of rnd, w&t.

Row 2 (WS): Purl to 1 st before m, w&t.

Row 3: Work in patt to 1 st before previous wrapped st, w&t.

Row 4: Purl to 1 st before previous wrapped st, w&t.

Rep Rows 3–4 until 6 (8, 8, 10) sts remain unworked between wrapped sts, ending with Row 4.

Row 5 (RS): Work in patt to wrapped st, w&t.

Row 6 (WS): Purl to wrapped st, w&t.

Row 7: Work in patt to double wrapped st, pick up wraps and knit tog with wrapped st, w&t.

Row 8: Purl to double wrapped st, pick up wraps and purl tog with wrapped st, w&t.

Rep Rows 7–8 until both sts before markers have been double wrapped.

Row 9: Work in patt to 1 st before end of rnd, pick up wraps and knit tog with wrapped st.

Set-up rnd: Knit to side m, remove m, pick up wraps and knit tog with wrapped st, k7 (8, 9, 10), pm for center of heel, knit to end of round.

Work 1 rnd even.

FOOT GUSSET

Rnd 1: Knit to 3 sts before center heel m, ssk, k1, sm, k1, k2tog, knit to end.

Rnd 2: Work in patt to 2 sts before m, k1, sl 1, sm, sl 1, k1, work in patt to end.

Rep these 2 rnds 3 more times. 32 (36, 40, 44) sts.

FOOT

Work even in patt as est until foot measures 7 (8, 9, 10)" / 18 (20.5, 23, 25.5) cm from back of heel, or 1" / 2.5cm less than desired foot length, ending with Rnd 4 of patt.

TOE

Set-up rnd: Work Rnd 1 of patt as est, placing toe shaping markers 8 (9, 10, 11) sts before and after the center heel marker. The first marker will be 4 sts after the beginning of rnd.

Dec Rnd 1: [Knit to 2 sts before m, ssk, sm, k2tog] twice, knit to end of round. 4 sts dec'd.

Dec Rnd 2: Work in patt as est.

Rep these 2 rnds twice more. 20 (24, 28, 32) sts.

Rearrange sts on two needles, with break at the toe shaping markers. Remove all markers. Graft rem sts together using Kitchener st.

PATTERN: LEFT SOCK

Work cuff and leg as for right sock.

ANKLE GUSSET

Rnd 1: Knit to m, sm, k1, m1 backward loop, knit to last st, m1 backward loop, k1.

Rnd 2: Work in patt as est, working a knit stitch into the m1 backward loop sts. Rep these 2 rnds 3 more times. 40 (44, 48, 52) sts.

Knit 1 rnd.

HEEL

Row 1 (RS): Work in patt to 1 st before m, w&t.

Row 2 (WS): Purl to 1 st before end of rnd, w&t.

Row 3: Work in patt to 1 st before previous wrapped st, w&t.

Row 4: Purl to 1 st before previous wrapped st, w&t.

Rep Rows 3–4 until 6 (8, 8, 10) sts remain unworked between wrapped sts, ending with Row 4.

Row 5 (RS): Work in patt to previous wrapped st, w&t.

Row 6 (WS): Purl to previous wrapped st, w&t.

Row 7: Work in patt to double wrapped st, pick up wraps and knit tog with wrapped st, w&t.
Row 8: Purl to double wrapped st, pick up wraps and purl tog with wrapped st, w&t.
Rep Rows 7–8 until both sts before markers have been double wrapped.

Row 9: Work in patt to 1 st before side m, pick up wraps and knit tog with wrapped st, sm, work in patt to end of rnd.

Set-up rnd: Pick up wraps and knit tog with wrapped st, k7 (8, 9, 10), pm for center of heel, knit to end, removing side m as you come to it.
Work 1 rnd even.

Work foot and toe as for right sock.

FINISHING

Block to even out stitches.

Using a spare piece of yarn, close up any holes at the corners of the heel short row shaping.

Weave in ends and trim.

RECOMMENDED VIEWING

☢ 28 Days Later

28 Days Later follows a group of survivors through the wastelands of Britain four weeks after an incurable (and highly contagious) virus called "Rage" is released among the populace. Part zombie movie, part *Outbreak*, and not quite implausible enough for comfort.

☢ Delicatessen

Not your usual post-apocalyptic movie, *Delicatessen* is a charming, dark comedy surrounding the goings-on at a boarding house above a delicatessen which, thanks to grave food shortages, primarily serves up the lodgers themselves—sort of a French, dystopian Sweeney Todd. The aesthetics are deliciously chilling, but *Delicatessen* manages to be amazingly lighthearted for a movie about cannibalism (but that's not too surprising from the director of *Amélie* and *Micmacs*.) Fair warning, there is some momentary inaccurate knitting (shudder!).

☢ Planet of the Apes

Yeah, you know how it ends, and Charlton Heston is cheesy as can be—but it's a classic!

☢ The Road

A man and his son trek through the ashy wastelands in hopes of finding something—anything—to keep them going. Seriously dismal. There's a book too, but with the film you get some well-done visuals and some nice handknits to go along with your misery.

☢ Children of Men

In a world where all women have become infertile, Clive Owen must sexily protect the last fetus in existence.

☢ Dr. Strangelove

A classic black comedy about the men who set the end of the world in motion. Also, bomb-riding!

☢ Zombieland

A little quirkier than your usual zombie apocalypse movie, and Woody Harrelson is as lovable as ever. The film follows a small group of survivors as they road trip to California in search of an amusement park reputed to be a zombie-free haven. Bill Murray shows up in a rather fine cameo.

☢ Shaun of the Dead

Another unique take on the typical zombie flick, *Shaun of the Dead* (get it? like *Dawn of the Dead?*) features the fantastic Simon-Pegg-and-Nick-Frost comedy combo and tells the story of a rather sad little man dealing with his crappy life and messed-up relationships … but also, there are zombies. Because, you know, he just didn't have enough problems yet.

☢ Firefly (TV series)

Perhaps it's not apocalyptic, exactly, but you get the feeling something mighty unpleasant must have happened to Earth-That-Was. Perhaps we would have found out if someone hadn't gotten a little too cancel-happy *coughFoxcough*. Regardless, the adventures of this much-beloved, ragtag band of Space-Pirate-Cowboys are not to be missed.

☢ Dollhouse (TV series)

What if you could download (and upload) the complete contents of someone's mind? What if you could program people to be whatever you wanted them to be … for a price? What if you could achieve immortality by hitching a ride in someone else's head? What if you were a saucy young lady who liked to kick a lot of ass, just the way Joss Whedon likes 'em? These answers and more on this week's episode of *Dollhouse*.

☢ The Walking Dead (TV series)

Zombies, duh!

KILL ALL HUMANS

You just HAD to have the newest iPhone.

Situation: We finally invented computers that are smarter than we are. Sure, it sounds like fun to have a Rosie the Robot around the house, but what if she decides she doesn't want to clean anymore? Luckily they're still susceptible to things like water and smelting. And maybe guns.

ALTERNATING CURRENT

Alexandra Tinsley

Feel the power! A positively electric cowl to give you a bit of a jolt, and perhaps help you blend in with your new robot overlords. Slouch it down for a cool cyber-babe look, or pull it up and add sunglasses for futuristic-incognito mode.

PATTERN NOTES

This pattern is knit flat, however, using a circular needle will be more comfortable than attempting to fit all the stitches on a straight needle. If you don't wish to deal with the provisional cast on, you can use a traditional cast on and bind off and seam the work closed instead (however you will not have a 3-D CC seam as shown.) For a wider cowl, simply work for longer before doing the bind off.

PATTERN

With CC, provisionally CO 91 sts.
Row 1 (CC): Purl.

Row 2 (MC): [K1, m1L, k4, s2kp, k4, m1R, k1] to end.

Row 3 (MC): Purl.
Rows 4–5 (MC): Rep Rows 2–3.

Row 6 (CC): [K1, m1L, k4, s2kp, k4, m1R, k1] to end.
Row 7 (CC): Purl.

Rep Rows 2–7 until piece measures 18" / 45.5cm, then rep Rows 2–3 once more.

FINISHING

Place the provisionally cast on stitches onto a spare needle, fold the work in half with WS facing each other and RS out, and using CC, work a 3-needle bind off. Block and weave in ends.

SIZE

One size

FINISHED MEASUREMENTS

Circumference: 19" / 48.5cm
Length: 16" / 40.5cm

MATERIALS

Black Trillium Fibre Studio Pebble Worsted (100% Superwash Merino Wool; 190 yds / 174m per 100g skein)

⚡ [MC] Inkwell; 1 skein

⚡ [CC] Lightning Bug; 1 skein

24-inch US #8 / 5mm circular needle, or size needed to obtain gauge
Spare #8 needle to use while working 3-needle bind off

Waste yarn for provisional cast on, yarn needle

GAUGE

18 sts and 28 rows = 4" / 10cm in St st

Gauge is not critical in this pattern, but a different gauge will affect the amount of yarn needed and size of finished item.

GROM-MITTS

Brenda K. B. Anderson

Keep your arms warm and protected while looking super cool in these extra-long mitts. Large metal grommets accentuate and modernize the cable panel that runs the length of these arm warmers. Everyone knows that grommets are like fancy jewelry during an apocalypse! And sometimes a girl wants to be fancy—even when she's fighting off killer robots.

PATTERN NOTES

These mitts are knit at a tighter gauge than normal to create a more elastic fabric. Because the rib pattern stitch is so stretchy it may be difficult to measure proper gauge.

The best way to check your gauge is to knit a few inches of the mitt following the pattern (through Round 20 of cable pattern), then check the width around your palm and bicep about 2–3" / 5–7.5cm above elbow. Sample should stretch to fit both areas. You may wish to save this sample of the mitt to use as practice when learning how to attach the eyelets, especially if you have never set an eyelet before.

These mitts are knit in the round from the top down. If you would like to make a shorter pair of mitts, work fewer repeats of the cable pattern. Two stitches will be

bound off in the center of each cable to leave a hole for the eyelet. On the next round 2 stitches will be cast on over the hole created by the BO sts. If your gauge is too loose, the holes at the center of each cable may be too large and the eyelets may slip out of place.

PATTERN: RIGHT MITT

ARM

CO 51 sts, pm and join to work in the round.

Rnds 1–4: [K3, p1] 2 times, pm, p3, k4, p4, pm, [k3, p1] 8 times.
Rnd 5: [K3, p1] 2 times, work Rnd 1 of Grom-mitts Cable chart between m, [k3, p1] 8 times.

Work as est until 6 repeats (120 rnds) of cable chart have been worked.

Work 4 more rnds, ending with Rnd 4 of cable patt.

RIGHT THUMB GUSSET

Rnd 1: [K3, p1] 2 times, work Rnd 5 of chart between m, [k3, p1] 2 times, k3, m1L, pm, k1, pm, m1R, [k3, p1] 5 times. 53 sts.

Rnd 2: [K3, p1] 2 times, work next rnd of chart between m, [k3, p1] 3 times, sm, m1L, knit to m, m1R, sm, p1, [k3, p1] 5 times. 2 sts inc'd in thumb gusset.

Rnd 3: [K3, p1] 2 times, work next rnd of chart between m, [k3, p1] 3 times, sm, knit to m, sm, p1, [k3, p1] 5 times.

Rnds 4–18: Rep Rnds 2-3 seven more times, then Rnd 3 again. 69 sts; 17 sts in thumb gusset.

SIZE

One size fits most women and teens. These mitts are very stretchy and will fit up to a 13" / 33cm bicep. Intended to be worn with 1–2" / 2.5–5cm of negative ease at hand and up to 6" / 15cm of negative ease at bicep.

FINISHED MEASUREMENTS

(slightly stretched)
Length: 21" / 53cm
Circumference: 7" / 18cm

MATERIALS

Zitron Ecco (100% superwash merino; 121 yds / 111m per 50g skein); color: Charcoal Gray #155; 3 skeins

Set of US #3 / 3.25mm dpns, or size needed to obtain gauge

Stitch markers, stitch holder or waste yarn, yarn needle

Sixteen 7/16" eyelets (also called grommets) and tools to attach eyelets (Suggested: Dritz brand "Extra-Large Eyelet Kit" in Zinc (Manufacturer # DR 660-65) and Dritz brand "Extra-Large Eyelets" in Zinc (Manufacturer # DR 661-65))

You need eyelets that have sharp teeth to grip the fabric. It's advisable to purchase a couple of extra eyelets to practice with on the gauge swatch.

Hammer and several sheets of paper, for setting eyelets

GAUGE

(also see Pattern Notes)
11-st cable panel measures 1.25" / 3 cm wide
28 sts / 31 rounds = 4" / 10 cm in [k3, p1] rib patt, stretched just enough to allow rib to lay flat. (Note that the purl columns are still not visible when stretched this small amount.)

Rnd 19: [K3, p1] 2 times, work next rnd of chart between m, [k3, p1] 3 times, remove m, place next 17 sts on holder for thumb, remove m, p1, [k3, p1] 5 times. 52 sts.

Rnd 20: [K3, p1] 2 times, work next rnd of chart between m, [k3, p1] 2 times, k3, p2tog, [k3, p1] 5 times. 51 sts.

Rnds 21–27: [K3, p1] 2 times, work next rnd of chart between m, [k3, p1] 8 times. At the end of Rnd 27, 8 full repeats plus 11 rnds of the cable chart have been worked.

Rnds 28-31: [K3, p1] 2 times, sm, p3, k4, p4, sm, [k3, p1] 8 times.

BO all sts in patt.

THUMB

Place thumb sts from stitch holder onto dpns.
Rnd 1: Join yarn, pick up and knit 2 sts where thumb meets hand, k17, k2tog. 18 sts.
Rnd 2: [K3, p1, k3, p2tog] 2 times. 16 sts.
Rnds 3–5: [K3, p1] 4 times.
BO all sts in patt.

PATTERN: LEFT MITT

Work as for Right Mitt until Thumb Gusset Shaping.

LEFT THUMB GUSSET

Rnd 1: [K3, p1] 2 times, work Rnd 5 of chart between m, [k3, p1] 6 times, k3, m1L, pm, k1, pm, m1R, k3, p1.

Rnd 2: [K3, p1] 2 times, work next rnd of chart between m, [k3, p1] 7 times, sm, m1L, knit to m, m1R, sm, p1, k3, p1. 2 sts inc'd.

Rnd 3: [K3, p1] 2 times, work next rnd of chart between m, [k3, p1] 7 times, sm, knit to m, sm, p1, k3, p1.

Rnds 4–18: Rep Rnds 2-3 seven more times, then Rnd 3 again. 69 sts; 17 sts in thumb gusset.

Rnd 19: [K3, p1] 2 times, work next rnd of chart between m, [k3, p1] 7 times, remove m, place next 17 sts on holder for thumb, remove m, p1, k3, p1. 52 sts.

Rnd 20: [K3, p1] 2 times, work next rnd of chart between m, [k3, p1] 6 times, k3, p2tog, k3, p1. 51 sts.

Rnds 21–27: [K3, p1] 2 times, work next rnd of chart between m, [k3, p1] 8 times. At the end of Rnd 27, 8 full repeats plus 11 rnds of the cable chart have been worked.

Rnds 28–31: [K3, p1] 2 times, sm, p3, k4, p4, sm, [k3, p1] 8 times.
BO all sts in patt.
Work Thumb as for Right Mitt.

FINISHING

Weave in ends. Use yarn tails near thumb to close hole between thumb and hand. Spray or wet block if desired.

Fold a few sheets of paper in half so that they measure about 4" / 10cm wide. Stuff this inside of the mitt to help stretch out the cable pattern when attaching the eyelets and to protect the underside of the mitt when you attach the eyelet. Attaching eyelets is easier when done on a cutting mat or thin cardboard on top of a hard floor. Attach 1 eyelet (grommet) to the center of each cable section (through BO hole), following the package directions.

GROM-MITTS CABLE

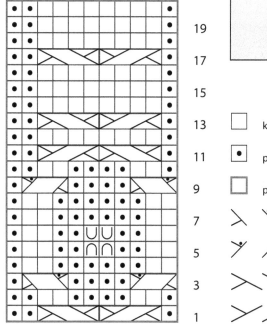

19
17
15
13
11
9
7
5
3
1

□	knit	⋒	bind off
•	purl	∪	cast on
□	pattern repeat		

⟩ ⟨ 2/1 LCp: sl 2 to cn, hold to front, p1, k2 from cn

⟩ ⟨ 2/1 RCp: sl 1 to cn, hold to back, k2, p1 from cn

⟩ ⟨ 2/2 LC: sl 2 to cn, hold to front, k2, k2 from cn

⟩ ⟨ 2/2 RC: sl 2 to cn, hold to back, k2, k2 from cn

CIRCUIT

SpillyJane

When the lights finally go out on civilization, we're going to need another power source. These mittens, with their mystical/technical motifs, are a reminder that the power has always been—and always will be—within each of us. Stylized versions of the symbols commonly used to represent our bodies' seven main chakra centers resonate within an Egyptian-style cartouche. The surrounding circuit board amplifies this generated power and puts it to the best possible use for the benefit all. Plug in.

PATTERN: LEFT MITTEN

CUFF

With MC, CO 64 sts, pm and join to work in the round.

Rnd 1: [K2 tbl, p2] to end.
Rep Rnd 1 nine more times.
Knit 2 rnds.

HAND

Work Rnds 1–23 of Left Mitten chart.

Rnd 24: Work chart to sts bordered in red. Using waste yarn, k10. Cut waste yarn. Transfer these 10 sts back to left needle and work chart to end.

Work Rnds 25–73 of chart. 20 sts rem.

Break yarns, leaving a long tail of MC. Graft the top of the mitten closed.

THUMB

Remove waste yarn and place the resulting 20 sts on dpns. Join MC.

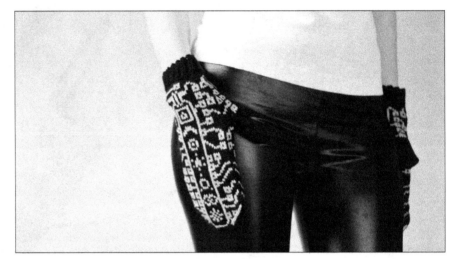

Rnd 1: Knit, picking up and knitting an additional 2 sts at either end of thumb hole. 24 sts.

Continue in St st with MC until thumb measures 0.5" / 1.5cm less than desired length.

SHAPE TOP

Rnd 1: [Skp, k8, k2tog] twice. 20 sts.
Rnd 2: [Skp, k6, k2tog] twice. 16 sts.
Rnd 3: [Skp, k4, k2tog] twice. 12 sts.

Rnd 4: [Skp, k2, k2tog] twice. 8 sts. Break yarn and graft top of thumb closed.

PATTERN: RIGHT MITTEN

Work same as Left Mitten, following Right Mitten chart.

FINISHING

Weave in ends. Place mitten beneath a damp tea towel and press with a hot iron to steam block.

SIZE

Women's Medium

FINISHED MEASUREMENTS

Palm circumference: 8" / 20.5cm

MATERIALS

Shibui Knits Sock (100% superwash merino wool; 191 yds / 175m per 50g skein)

⧗ [MC] Abyss; 1 skein

⧗ [CC] Sky; 1 skein

Set of US #2 / 2.75mm dpns, or size needed to obtain gauge

Stitch marker, waste yarn, yarn needle

GAUGE

32 sts and 32 rnds = 4" / 10cm in stranded colorwork patt

LEFT MITTEN CHART

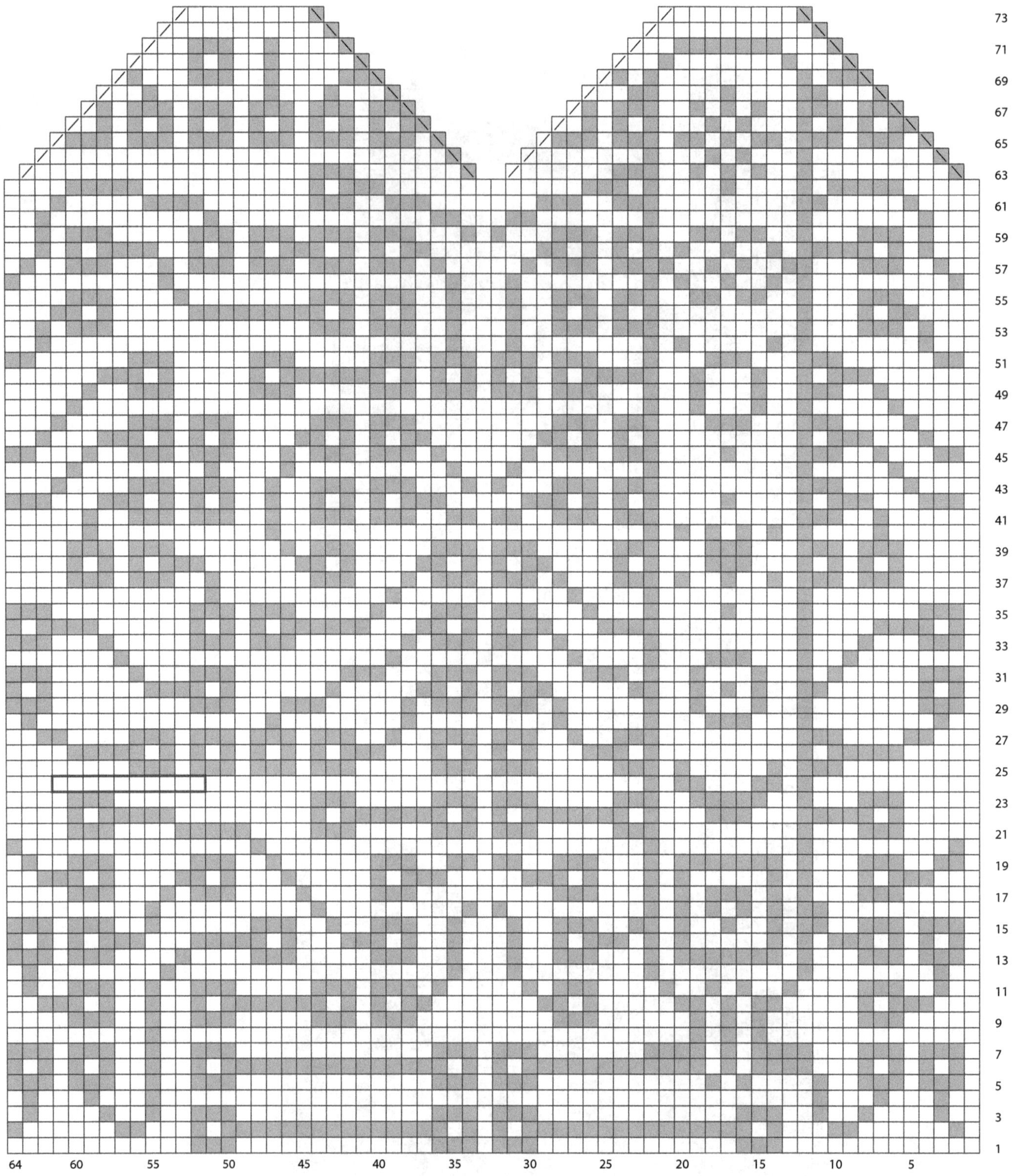

- knit MC
- knit CC
- skp with MC
- k2tog with MC
- skp with CC
- k2tog with CC
- thumb placement

RIGHT MITTEN CHART

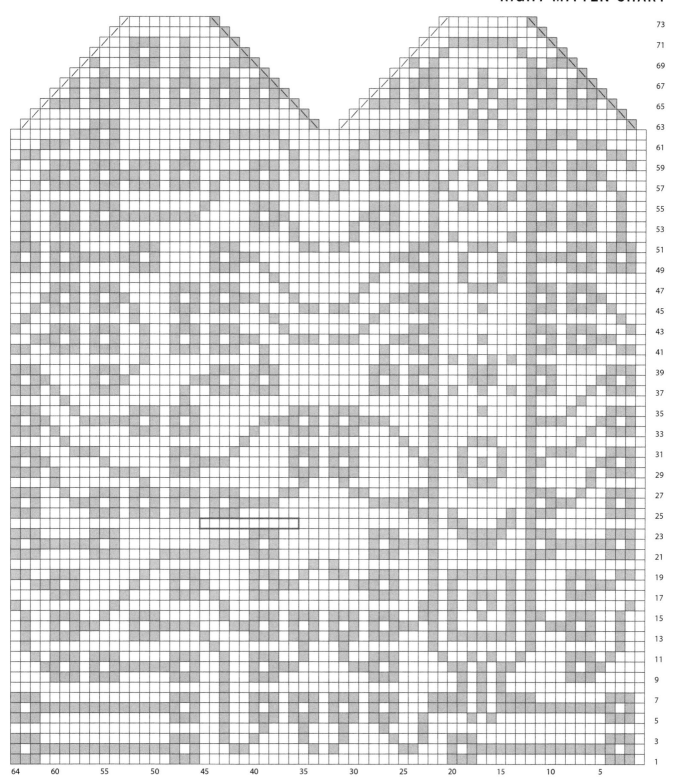

TECHNOLOGICA

Alexandra Tinsley

This sassy sweater is what "daughter Judy" would wear if she had to go kick some robot overlord ass ... or go to a rave. Either one, really.

PATTERN NOTES

Sweater is knit in the round from the bottom up, incorporating waist shaping at the back waist, a slit on the upper chest, raglan sleeve shaping, and a mock turtleneck.

PATTERN

LOWER BODY

With circular needle, CO 144 (164, 184, 204, 224, 244, 264) sts. Pm and join to work in the round. Work in St st for 2.75 (2.75, 2.75, 3, 3, 3)" / 7 (7, 7, 7.5, 7.5, 7.5, 7.5)cm.

Shape waist:
Next rnd: K66 (76, 86, 96, 106, 116, 126), pm for side, k27 (30, 34, 37, 40, 44, 47), pm for waist shaping, k24 (28, 30, 34, 38, 40, 44), pm for waist shaping, knit to end.

Dec Rnd: Knit to 2 sts before first waist shaping m, ssk, sm, knit to next m, sm, k2tog, knit to end. 2 sts dec'd.
Rep Dec Rnd on every 2nd (2nd, 2nd, 2nd, 3rd, 3rd, 3rd) rnd 21 (21, 21, 21, 15, 15, 15) more times. 100 (120, 140, 160, 192, 212, 232) sts.

Work 21 rnds even.

Inc Rnd: Knit to first waist shaping m, m1R, sm, knit to next m, sm, m1L, knit to end. 2 sts inc'd.
Rep Inc Rnd on every 2nd (2nd, 2nd, 2nd, 3rd, 3rd, 3rd) rnd 15 (15, 15, 15, 9, 9, 9) more times. 132 (152, 172, 192, 212, 232, 252) sts.

Removing the two waist shaping m on next rnd, work even until piece measures 16.5 (16.5, 16.5, 17, 17, 17, 17.5)" / 42 (42, 42, 43, 43, 43, 44.5)cm from CO.

YOKE

Sizes XS (S, M) only:
Next rnd: Knit to side m, sm, CO 40 (46, 54) sts for sleeve, pm for raglan, knit to end of rnd, sm, CO 40 (46, 54) sts for sleeve, pm for raglan and new beg of rnd. 212 (244, 280) sts.

Sizes – (–, –, L, XL, 2X, 3X) only:
Next rnd: Knit to – (–, –, 1, 3, 4, 5) st(s) before side m, BO – (–, –, 2, 6, 8, 10) sts for underarm, removing m, knit to last – (–, –, 1, 3, 4, 5) st(s), BO – (–, –, 2, 6, 8, 10) sts, removing m. – (–, –, 94, 100, 108, 116) sts rem for front and same number for back.

Next rnd: Knit to first BO, pm for raglan, CO – (–, –, 58, 64, 68, 72) sts for sleeve, pm for raglan, knit to second BO, pm for raglan, CO – (–, –, 58, 64, 68, 72) sts for sleeve, pm for raglan and new beg of rnd. – (–, –, 304, 328, 352, 376) sts.

All sizes:
Knit 1 rnd.

Size XS only:
Dec Rnd 1: [K1, k2tog, knit to 3 sts before next m, ssk, k1, sm] 4 times. 8 sts dec'd.
Knit 1 rnd.
Rep Dec Rnd 1.
Knit 2 rnds.
Rep the last 5 rnds 2 more times.
Rep Dec Rnd 1. 156 sts: 52 sts each back and front, and 26 each sleeve.
Knit 1 rnd.

Make front slit (size XS):
Next rnd: K1, k2tog, k6, BO 34 sts, knit to 3 sts before next m, ssk, k1, sm, [k1, k2tog, knit to 3 sts before next m, ssk, k1, sm] 3 times.
Next rnd: Knit to bound-off sts, CO 34 sts, knit to end. 148 sts: 50 sts each back and front, and 24 each sleeve.
Knit 1 rnd.

SIZES

Women's XS (S, M, L, XL, 2XL); shown in size XS

Intended to be worn with 1–3" / 2.5–7.5cm of negative ease

FINISHED MEASUREMENTS

Bust: 26.5 (30.5, 34.5, 38.5, 42.5, 46.5, 50.5)" / 66 (76, 86, 96, 106, 116, 126)cm

MATERIALS

Austermann Merino Silk (70% merino, 22% silk, 8% cashmere; 125 yds / 115m per 50g skein); color: 0612; 5 (7, 7, 8, 9, 10, 11) skeins

24- or 32-inch US #7 / 4.5mm circular needle, or size needed to obtain gauge
Set of US #7 / 4.5mm dpns

Stitch markers, yarn needle

GAUGE

20 sts and 31 rows = 4" / 10cm in St st

Continue raglan shaping (size XS):
Change to dpns when necessary.
Rep Dec Rnd 1.
Knit 1 rnd.
Rep Dec Rnd 1.
Knit 2 rnds.
Rep the last 5 rnds 4 more times. 68 sts: 30 each back and front, and 4 each sleeve.
Dec Rnd 2: [K1, k2tog, knit to 3 sts before next m, ssk, k1, sm, knit to next m, sm] 2 times. 4 sts dec'd.
Knit 1 rnd.
Rep Dec Rnd 2. 60 sts: 26 each back and front, and 4 each sleeve.

Size S only:
Dec Rnd 1: [K1, k2tog, knit to 3 sts before next m, ssk, k1, sm] 4 times. 8 sts dec'd.
Knit 1 rnd.
Rep Dec Rnd 1.
Knit 2 rnds.
Rep the last 5 rnds 3 more times.
Rep Dec Rnd 1.
Knit 1 rnd.
Rep the last 2 rnds once more. 164 sts: 56 each back and front, and 26 each sleeve.

Make front slit (size S):
Next rnd: K1, k2tog, k7, BO 36 sts, knit to 3 sts before next m, ssk, k1, sm, [k1, k2tog, knit to 3 sts before next m, ssk, k1, sm] 3 times.

Next rnd: Knit to bound-off sts, CO 36 sts, knit to end. 156 sts: 54 each back and front, and 24 each sleeve.

Continue raglan shaping (size S):
Change to dpns when necessary.
Rep Dec Rnd 1 on next rnd, then every other rnd 9 more times. 76 sts: 34 each back and front, and 4 each sleeve.
Knit 1 rnd.
Dec Rnd 2: [K1, k2tog, knit to 3 sts before next m, ssk, k1, sm, knit to next m, sm] 2 times. 4 sts dec'd.
Rep Dec Rnd 2 on every other rnd 2 more times. 64 sts: 28 each back and front, and 4 each sleeve.

Sizes – (–, M, L, XL, 2X, 3X) only:
Dec Rnd 1: [K1, k2tog, knit to 3 sts before next m, ssk, k1, sm] 4 times. 8 sts dec'd.
Rep Dec Rnd 1 on every rnd – (–, 0, 0, 2, 4, 6) more times, then on every other rnd – (–, 12, 15, 15, 15, 16) times. – (–, 176, 176, 184, 192, 192) sts: – (–, 60, 62, 64, 68, 70) each back and front, and – (–, 28, 26, 28, 28, 26) each sleeve.
Knit 1 rnd.

Make front slit (sizes M–3X):
Next rnd: K1, k2tog, k – (–, 8, 8, 8, 9, 9), BO – (–, 38, 40, 42, 44, 46) sts, knit to 3 sts before next m, ssk, k1, sm, [k1, k2tog, knit to 3 sts before next m, ssk, k1, sm] 3 times.

Next rnd: Knit to bound-off sts, CO – (–, 38, 40, 42, 44, 46) sts, knit to end. – (–, 168, 168, 176, 184, 184) sts: – (–, 58, 60, 62, 66, 68) each back and front, and – (–, 26, 24, 26, 26, 24) each sleeve.

Continue raglan shaping (sizes M–3X):
Change to dpns when necessary.
Rep Dec Rnd 1 on next rnd, then every other rnd – (–, 10, 9, 10, 10, 9) more times. – (–, 80, 88, 88, 96, 104) sts: – (–, 36, 40, 40, 44, 48) each back and front, and 4 each sleeve.
Knit 1 rnd.
Dec Rnd 2: [K1, k2tog, knit to 3 sts before next m, ssk, k1, sm, knit to next m, sm] 2 times. 4 sts dec'd.
Rep Dec Rnd 2 on every other rnd – (–, 2, 3, 2, 3, 4) more times. – (–, 68, 72, 76, 80, 84) sts: – (–, –, 30, 32, 34, 36, 38) each back and front, and 4 each sleeve.

COLLAR

All sizes:
Work even on rem sts for 2" / 5cm.
BO using a stretchy method.

FINISHING

Weave in all ends and block gently.

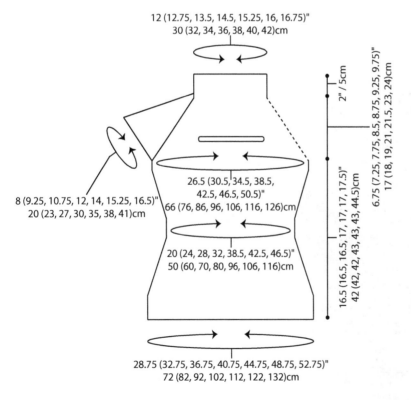

12 (12.75, 13.5, 14.5, 15.25, 16, 16.75)"
30 (32, 34, 36, 38, 40, 42)cm

2" / 5cm

6.75 (7.25, 7.75, 8.5, 8.75, 9.25, 9.75)"
17 (18, 19, 21, 21.5, 23, 24)cm

26.5 (30.5, 34.5, 38.5, 42.5, 46.5, 50.5)"
66 (76, 86, 96, 106, 116, 126)cm

8 (9.25, 10.75, 12, 14, 15.25, 16.5)"
20 (23, 27, 30, 35, 38, 41)cm

16.5 (16.5, 16.5, 17, 17, 17, 17.5)"
42 (42, 42, 43, 43, 43, 44.5)cm

20 (24, 28, 32, 38.5, 42.5, 46.5)"
50 (60, 70, 80, 96, 106, 116)cm

28.75 (32.75, 36.75, 40.75, 44.75, 48.75, 52.75)"
72 (82, 92, 102, 112, 122, 132)cm

CYBER DREADS

Alexandra Tinsley

Complete your cyber-punky aesthetic with these super easy faux dreads (called dreadfalls), made from a very familiar material!

TUTORIAL

1. Figure out approximately how long you want your falls. Cut the yarn into strips that are slightly longer than twice the desired length (as shown, falls are 13" / 33cm and yarn was cut into 29" / 74cm strips).

2. Separate these strands into two batches.

3. Fold a strand in half and push the looped end through an elastic hair tie. Pull the loose ends through the looped end and pull snugly to attach it to the elastic. Repeat this process until you've got one batch of strands on one hair tie. They should take up about two-thirds of the hair tie ... really scrunch 'em! If you're running out of real estate, you can attach them two at a time. You want to cram as many on there as possible to make sure your falls are nice and lush.

4. Repeat with the second hair tie and the second batch of yarn.

5. Felting/Fulling: (You don't HAVE to felt your falls, if you like the way they look now. But it will give them a nice, dense, matted-hair look and make them a bit sturdier. If you do want to felt, trust me and do it by hand. If you put these babies in the washer you're probably just going to get a solid wad of wool.) Fill up a sink or bucket with hot water (as hot as you can comfortably stand—don't burn yourself!) and soap. Fill up another sink or bucket with ice water. Holding onto the elastics so they don't get too painfully tangled, dunk them in the hot water and knead. Don't be gentle! Wail on 'em like they stole something from your mama. Then, when you get bored, lift them out, squeeze some of the extra water out, and plunge them into the ice water. You can almost feel the fibers contract in on themselves like "HOLY CRAP THAT'S COLD." Keep alternating hot and cold until they are felted as desired. Keep an eye on them to make sure the strands aren't sticking together too badly—they definitely WILL stick together but you want those bonds to be weak enough to break apart later.

6. When you're done, squeeze out the excess water and roll them up in a towel. Then figure out where in your house it would be most alarming for someone to encounter sodden, disembodied dread-locks and hang them up there to dry.

7. Once they're dry, go through and separate any strands that have melded with their neighbors. You should be able to yank them apart, as long as you didn't get overzealous during the felting process. You can now add other sorts of goodies to your falls, if you want—like glow in the dark jelly yarn, or ribbon, or feathers, or wire ... get creative!

HOW TO WEAR

1. If you want to use a headband or goggles, put those around your neck before you attach the falls.

2. Put your hair in either high, perky pigtails or pigtail buns using regular hair ties (you'll need to experiment with what works best on your hair.)

3. Wrap the base of the bun/tail (where you've already got a hair tie) first with the yarn-covered portion of the hair tie, and then (keeping the dreads out of your way with your magical third hand) wrap the rest of the tie around and around until it's snug. You'll probably want to reinforce things with a few bobby pins.

4. Flip the dreads over so the buns/tails are concealed and arrange to your liking.

5. Rock your cybery 'do.

SIZE

One size

MATERIALS

Colinette Point 5 (100% wool; 54 yds / 49m per 100g skein); color: Neptune; 1 skein

Any chunky, felt-able yarn will work, but thick and thin looks best. Additional skeins may be used for thicker or longer dreads.

Yummy Yarns Glow Jelly Yarn Fine (100% vinyl; 85 yds / 78m per 200g ball); color: Green Peppermint, 1 ball

Miscellaneous bits of lace, ribbon, strips of tulle or fabric—anything that catches your fancy!

2 seamless elastic hair ties

MISCELLANEOUS MAYHEM

Epidemic? Angry race of genetically engineered clone slaves? Ran out of oil? Zombies? There are just so many ways to go.

Situation: There are way too many apocalyptic scenarios to cover each one in detail, but luckily your wardrobe needs will often be the same: you need to kick ass, take names, find food, and look awesome.

SURVIVOR

Mara Marzocchi

Come the chaos, some folks will need more than the leathers-and-feathers look. These socks have the look of a survivor who has felt the zombies' claws and lived to tell about it … probably.

PATTERN NOTES

Toe-up construction with a short row heel.

PATTERN

TOE

Using Turkish method, CO 24 (32) sts divided evenly over 2 needles: 12 (16) for instep and 12 (16) for sole.

Rnd 1: Knit.
Rnd 2: [K1, RLI, knit to last st on needle, LLI, k1] twice. 4 sts inc'd.
Rep these 2 rnds 7 (11) more times. 56 (80) sts: 28 (40) for instep and 28 (40) for sole.

FOOT

Next rnd: Work Right or Left chart for your size over 28 (40) instep sts, knit all sole sts.

Cont as set until sock measures 1.75 (2)" / 4.5 (5)cm less than desired length, switching to St st on instep after chart is complete. (If chart is not complete before you reach the required length, just make a note of the last rnd worked so you can come back to it after the heel.)

HEEL

Heel is worked over 28 (40) sole sts only. Work 28 (40) instep sts, then set aside on one or two needles while you work heel over rem sts.

Row 1 (RS): Knit to last st, w&t.
Row 2 (WS): Purl to last st, w&t.

Row 3: Knit to 1 st before previous wrapped st, w&t.
Row 4: Purl to 1 st before previous wrapped st, w&t.
Rep Rows 3–4 until 12 (14) sts rem unwrapped in center of heel.

Next row (RS): Knit to previous wrapped st, w&t.
Next row (WS): Purl to previous wrapped st, w&t.

Next row: Knit to double-wrapped st, pick up and knit both wraps tog with st, w&t.
Next row: Purl to double-wrapped st, pick up and purl both wraps tog with st, w&t.
Rep the last 2 rows until only one double-wrapped st remains at each end of heel.

Next row: Knit to last st, pick up both wraps and knit tog with st.

Resume working on all sts.

Next rnd: Pick up st under last st in rnd (the st below the st you just knit with its wraps) and knit it tog with the first st on the instep. (This helps prevent a hole where the heel meets the instep). Work across instep to last st, pick up st below the first st of the heel (the one below the st with two wraps) and knit tog. Pick up wraps on first heel st and knit tog with st, knit to end of rnd.

LEG

Work even for 2" / 5cm (or desired length).

CUFF

Work Rnds 1–23 of Cuff chart once, then rep Rnd 23 twenty more times. BO all sts in patt using your preferred stretchy method.

FINISHING

Weave in ends and block.

SIZES

S (L); shown in size S

To fit foot circumference: 8 (10)" / 20.5 (25.5)cm

FINISHED MEASUREMENTS

Foot circumference: 6.5 (9.5)" / 16.5 (23.5)cm

MATERIALS

Play At Life Fiber Arts Boundless Sock (75% merino, 25% nylon; 460 yds / 421m per 100g skein); color: Copperpot; 1 (2) skeins

Set of US #1 / 2.25mm dpns, or size needed to obtain gauge

Yarn needle

GAUGE

34 sts and 40 rows = 4" / 10cm in St st

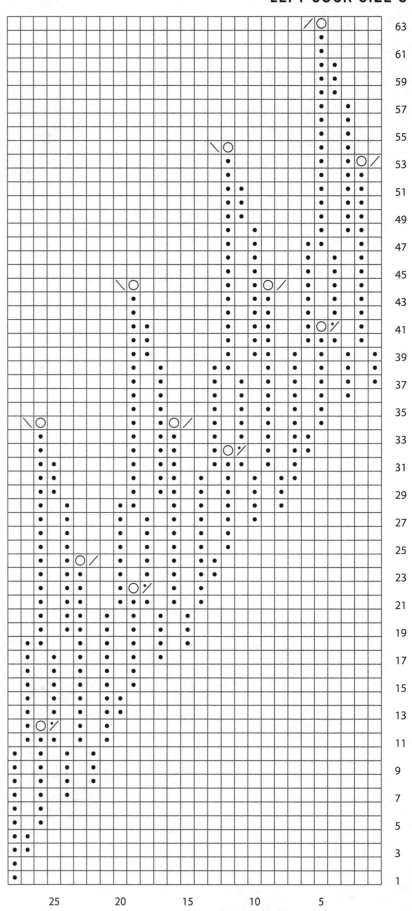

knit

purl

yo

ssk

k2tog

p2tog tbl

p2tog

pattern repeat

RIGHT SOCK SIZE S

CUFF (BOTH SIZES)

LEFT SOCK SIZE L

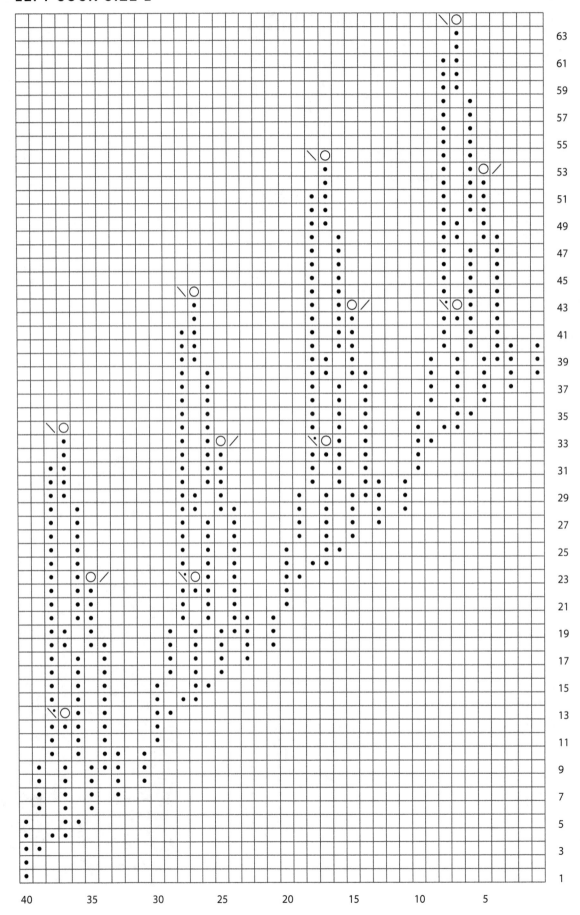

RIGHT SOCK SIZE L

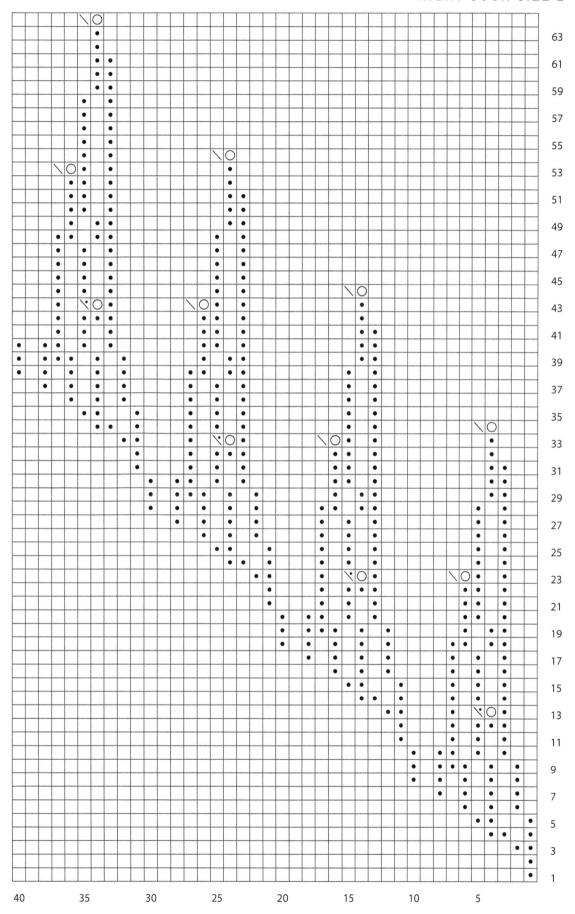

OH BONDAGE!

Alexandra Tinsley

Some people think that little girls should be seen and not heard. But I think ... wait, why are you looking at me like that? ....aacck no! NO! Nooooogurrrgggglss ......

PATTERN NOTES

Cowl is worked from the top down, starting with garter stitch in the round before dividing stitches for the front and back flaps, which are worked separately. Straps are sewn on after the cowl is completed.

STITCHES AND TECHNIQUES

GARTER STITCH (IN THE ROUND)

Rnd 1: Knit.
Rnd 2: Purl.

PATTERN

CO 46 sts, pm and join in the round, being careful not to twist.

Work in garter stitch for 28 rnds.

FLAPS

Break yarn. Put first 11 and last 12 sts of rnd on waste yarn or stitch holder (they can be on the same holder together, to equal 23 sts held total.)

Working on the other 23 sts, rejoin yarn with WS facing.

Set-up row (WS): [P1, k1] to last st, p1.
Inc Row (RS): K1, m1, work in est rib to last st, m1, k1. 2 sts inc'd.

Working inc'd sts into rib, rep Inc Row on every RS row 3 more times, or until the corners of the flap just reach to your armpits. BO.

Move the sts that are on waste yarn or holder back on the needle. Work the second flap as the first.

FINISHING

Weave in all ends and block gently. Try the cowl on and experiment with the straps to determine where to place them—try using large safety pins to hold them where you like them. Sew the straps into place.

SIZE

One size

FINISHED MEASUREMENTS

Height: 9.5" / 24cm
Width (at neck): 22" / 56cm

MATERIALS

Malabrigo Rasta (100% merino wool; 90 yds / 82m per 150g skein); color: Oxido; 2 skeins.

20-inch US #15 / 10mm circular needle.

1 stitch marker, large stitch holder or waste yarn, yarn needle

2 purse straps long enough to fit from the front of the cowl, under your arms and meet at the back of the cowl (can be purchased at most major craft stores)

GAUGE

8.5 sts and 19 rows = 4" / 10 cm in garter stitch

DITCH THE TECH

Jennette Cross

This sweater was inspired by the *Dollhouse* Thoughtpocalypse. Once the world ends the long length and sleeves will be great for keeping warm on those cold nights after we have to abandon technology. You know, because anything that transmits may be able to replace our personalities and turn us into a mindless army.

PATTERN NOTES

This pullover is knit from the top down, starting with the collar, which is worked shortways. Stitches are picked up along the long side and the yoke is started with short rows. After the short rows are completed there are increases on the front edges to begin creating the curve for the scoop neck.

After the curve increases are complete the stitches at the bottom of the curve are cast on and the yoke is worked in the round to the sleeve divide, after which it is fairly straightforward to the hem.

The hems, neckline, and collar are edged with single crochet to provide some stability and give a unified appearance.

Some of the curl at the hems can be tamed with blocking.

PATTERN

COLLAR

With circular needle, CO 32 (32, 38, 38, 44, 44, 50, 50) sts. Knit 1 row.

Set-up row (WS): Sl 1 wyif, [k1, p4, k1] to last st, k1.

Work Rows 1–4 of Collar Lace chart 49 (56, 60, 66, 68, 73, 80, 83) times, then work Rows 1–3 once more.

Set-up row for yoke (WS): Sl 1, [p1, insert left needle into 2 sts on right needle and p2tog] to end. 1 st remains on right needle. Do not fasten off and do not turn. With WS of collar facing, pick up and knit 101 (115, 123, 135, 139, 149, 163, 169) sts along long edge of collar (1 st in each slipped selvage st). 102 (116, 124, 136, 140, 150, 164, 170) sts.

YOKE

Note: WS of collar is RS of yoke.

Short Row Shaping:

Set-up row (WS): Sl 1, p17 (18, 17, 21, 22, 25, 28, 30), pm, k1, p4, k1, pm, p10 (12, 14, 14, 14, 14, 14, 14), pm, k1, p4, k1, pm, p22 (30, 36, 40, 42, 46, 54, 56), pm, k1, p4, k1, pm, p10 (12, 14, 14, 14, 14, 14, 14), pm, k1, p4, k1, turn. 18 (19, 18, 22, 23, 26, 29, 31) sts rem unworked.

Row 1 (RS): Yo, pm, work Row 1 of Raglan Lace over 6 sts, sm, yo, [knit to m, yo, sm, work Row 1 of Raglan Lace over 6 sts, sm, yo] 3 times, ssk, turn. 16 (17, 16, 20, 21, 24, 27, 29) sts rem unworked.

Row 2: Sl 1, [purl to m, sm, work next row of Raglan Lace, sm] 4 times, p1, p2tog, turn. 16 (17, 16, 20, 21, 24, 27, 29) sts rem unworked.

SIZES

Women's XS (S, M, L, XL, 2X, 3X, 4X); shown in size S

Intended to be worn with 1" / 2.5cm of positive ease.

FINISHED MEASUREMENTS

Bust: 34 (37, 42.25, 46, 49.25, 53, 58.25, 62)" / 85 (93, 105.5, 115, 123, 133, 145.5, 155)cm

MATERIALS

Cephalopod Yarns Bugga! (70% superwash merino, 20% cashmere, 10% nylon; 412 yds / 377m per 113g skein); color: Fig Eater Y051; 4 (5, 5, 6, 6, 7, 7, 8) skeins

US #3 / 3.25mm circular needle, or size needed to obtain gauge in length appropriate for body circumference Set of US #3 / 3.25mm dpns or long circular needles for Magic Loop on sleeves

US size F / 3.75mm crochet hook

Stitch markers, stitch holders, yarn needle

GAUGE

25 sts and 37 rows = 4" / 10 cm in St st

Both stitch and row gauge are important in this pattern.

COLLAR LACE CHART

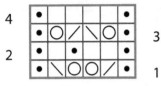

RAGLAN LACE CHART

	RS: knit; WS: purl
•	RS: purl; WS: knit
O	yo
V	RS: sl 1 wyib; WS: sl1 wyif
\	ssk
/	k2tog
	pattern repeat

Row 3: Sl 1, [knit to m, yo, sm, work next row of Raglan Lace, sm, yo] 4 times, knit to 1 st before previous turn, ssk, turn.

Row 4: Sl 1, [purl to m, sm, work next row of Raglan Lace, sm] 4 times, purl to 1 st before previous turn, p2tog, turn.

Rep Rows 3–4 15 (16, 15, 19, 20, 23, 26, 28) times more. 204 (224, 226, 262, 272, 300, 332, 350) sts; 18 (19, 18, 22, 23, 26, 29, 31) each front, 56 (66, 70, 82, 86, 96, 110, 116) in back, 44 (48, 48, 56, 58, 64, 70, 74) each sleeve, and 4 Raglan Lace sections of 6 sts each.

Curve Yoke Section:
Size XS only:
Row 1 (RS): Sl 1, k1, m1L, [knit to m, yo, sm, work Raglan Lace, sm, yo] 4 times, knit to last 2 sts, m1R, k2. 8 raglan sts and 2 neck sts inc'd.

Row 2: Sl 1, [purl to m, sm, work Raglan Lace, sm] 4 times, purl to last st, k1.

Row 3: Sl 1, [knit to m, yo, sm, work Raglan Lace, sm, yo] 4 times, knit to end. 8 raglan sts inc'd.

Row 4: Rep Row 2.
Rows 5–8: Rep Rows 1–4.
Rows 9–10: Rep Rows 1–2.

Row 11: Sl 1, k1, m1L, [knit to 2 sts before m, ssk, yo, sm, work Raglan Lace, sm, yo, k2tog] 4 times, knit to last 2 sts, m1R, k2. 2 neck sts inc'd.

Row 12: Rep Row 2.
Row 13: Rep Row 1.
Row 14: Rep Row 2.
Row 15: Rep Row 11.
Row 16: Rep Row 2.

264 sts: 30 each front, 68 in back, 56 each sleeve, and 4 Raglan Lace sections of 6 sts each.

Size S only:
Row 1 (RS): Sl 1, k1, m1L, [knit to m, yo, sm, work Raglan Lace, sm, yo] 4 times, knit to last 2 sts, m1R, k2. 8 raglan sts and 2 neck sts inc'd.

Row 2: Sl 1, [purl to m, sm, work Raglan Lace, sm] 4 times, purl to last st, k1.

Row 3: Sl 1, [knit to m, yo, sm, work Raglan Lace, sm, yo] 4 times, knit to end. 8 raglan sts inc'd.

Row 4: Rep Row 2.
Rows 5–8: Rep Rows 1–4.
Rows 9–10: Rep Rows 1–2.

Row 11: Sl 1, k1, m1L, [knit to 2 sts before m, ssk, yo, sm, work Raglan Lace, sm, yo, k2tog] 4 times, knit to last 2 sts, m1R, k2. 2 neck sts inc'd.

Row 12: Rep Row 2.
Row 13: Rep Row 1.
Row 14: Rep Row 2.
Row 15: Rep Row 11.
Row 16: Rep Row 2.
Row 17: Rep Row 1.

Row 18: Sl 1, p1, m1Rp, [purl to m, sm, work Raglan Lace, sm] 4 times, purl to last 2 sts, m1Lp, p1, k1. 2 neck sts inc'd.

296 sts: 34 each front, 80 in back, 62 each sleeve, and 4 Raglan Lace sections of 6 sts each.

Size M only:
Row 1 (RS): Sl 1, k1, m1L, [knit to m, yo, sm, work Raglan Lace, sm, yo] 4 times, knit to last 2 sts, m1R, k2. 8 raglan sts and 2 neck sts inc'd.

Row 2: Sl 1, [purl to m, sm, work Raglan Lace, sm] 4 times, purl to last st, k1.

Row 3: Sl 1, [knit to m, yo, sm, work Raglan Lace, sm, yo] 4 times, knit to end. 8 raglan sts inc'd.

Row 4: Rep Row 2.
Rows 5–12: Rep Rows 1–4 two times.
Rows 13–14: Rep Rows 1–2.

Row 15: Sl 1, k1, m1L, [knit to 2 sts before m, ssk, yo, sm, work Raglan Lace, sm, yo, k2tog] 4 times, knit to last 2 sts, m1R, k2. 2 neck sts inc'd.

Row 16: Rep Row 2.
Row 17: Rep Row 1.
Row 18: Rep Row 2.
Row 19: Rep Row 15.
Row 20: Rep Row 2.
Row 21: Rep Row 1.

Row 22: Sl 1, p1, m1Rp, [purl to m, sm, work Raglan Lace, sm] 4 times, purl to last 2 sts, m1Lp, p1, k1. 2 neck sts inc'd.

316 sts: 36 each front, 88 in back, 66 each sleeve, and 4 Raglan Lace sections of 6 sts each.

Size L only:
Row 1 (RS): Sl 1, k1, m1L, [knit to m, yo, sm, work Raglan Lace, sm, yo] 4 times, knit to last 2 sts, m1R, k2. 8 raglan sts and 2 neck sts inc'd.

Row 2: Sl 1, [purl to m, sm, work Raglan Lace, sm] 4 times, purl to last st, k1.

Row 3: Sl 1, [knit to m, yo, sm, work Raglan Lace, sm, yo] 4 times, knit to end. 8 raglan sts inc'd.

Row 4: Rep Row 2.
Rows 5–12: Rep Rows 1–4 two times.
Rows 13–14: Rep Rows 1–2.

Row 15: Sl 1, k1, m1L, [knit to 2 sts before m, ssk, yo, sm, work Raglan Lace, sm, yo, k2tog] 4 times, knit to last 2 sts, m1R, k2. 2 neck sts inc'd.

Row 16: Rep Row 2.
Row 17: Rep Row 1.
Row 18: Rep Row 2.
Row 19: Rep Row 15.
Row 20: Rep Row 2.
Row 21: Rep Row 1.

Row 22: Sl 1, p1, m1Rp, [purl to m, sm, work Raglan Lace, sm] 4 times, purl to last 2 sts, m1Lp, p1, k1. 2 neck sts inc'd.

352 sts: 40 each front, 100 in back, 74 each sleeve, and 4 Raglan Lace sections of 6 sts each.

Size XL only:
Row 1 (RS): Sl 1, k1, m1L, [knit to m, yo, sm, work Raglan Lace, sm, yo] 4 times, knit to last 2 sts, m1R, k2. 8 raglan sts and 2 neck sts inc'd.

Row 2: Sl 1, [purl to m, sm, work Raglan Lace, sm] 4 times, purl to last st, k1.

Row 3: Sl 1, [knit to m, yo, sm, work Raglan Lace, sm, yo] 4 times, knit to end. 8 raglan sts inc'd.

Row 4: Rep Row 2.
Rows 5–12: Rep Rows 1–4 two times.
Rows 13–16: Rep Rows 1–2 two times.

Row 17: Sl 1, k1, m1L, [knit to 2 sts before m, ssk, yo, sm, work Raglan Lace, sm, yo, k2tog] 4 times, knit to last 2 sts, m1R, k2. 2 neck sts inc'd.

Row 18: Rep Row 2.
Rows 19–20: Rep Rows 1–2.
Row 21: Rep Row 17.

Row 22: Rep Row 2.
Row 23: Rep Row 1.
Row 24: Rep Row 22.

372 sts: 43 each front, 106 in back, 78 each sleeve, 4 Raglan Lace sections of 6 sts each.

Size 2X only:
Row 1 (RS): Sl 1, k1, m1L, [knit to m, yo, sm, work Raglan Lace, sm, yo] 4 times, knit to last 2 sts, m1R, k2. 8 raglan sts and 2 neck sts inc'd.

Row 2: Sl 1, [purl to m, sm, work Raglan Lace, sm] 4 times, purl to last st, k1.

Row 3: Sl 1, [knit to m, yo, sm, work Raglan Lace, sm, yo] 4 times, knit to end. 8 raglan sts inc'd.

Row 4: Rep Row 2.
Rows 5–12: Rep Rows 1–4 two times.
Rows 13–18: Rep Rows 1–2 three times.
Row 19: Rep Row 1.

Row 20: Sl 1, p1, m1Rp, [purl to m, sm, work Raglan Lace, sm] 4 times, purl to last 2 sts, m1Lp, p1, k1. 2 neck sts inc'd.
Row 21: Rep Row 1.
Row 22: Rep Row 20.

Row 23: Sl 1, k1, m1L, [knit to 2 sts before m, ssk, yo, sm, work Raglan Lace, sm, yo, k2tog] 4 times, knit to last 2 sts, m1R, k2. 2 neck sts inc'd.
Row 24: Rep Row 20.

412 sts: 49 each front, 118 in back, 86 each sleeve, and 4 Raglan Lace sections of 6 sts each.

Sizes 3X (4X) only:
Row 1 (RS): Sl 1, k1, m1L, [knit to m, yo, sm, work Raglan Lace, sm, yo] 4 times, knit to last 2 sts, m1R, k2. 8 raglan sts and 2 neck sts inc'd.

Row 2: Sl 1, [purl to m, sm, work Raglan Lace, sm] 4 times, purl to last st, k1.

Row 3: Sl 1, [knit to m, yo, sm, work Raglan Lace, sm, yo] 4 times, knit to end. 8 raglan sts inc'd.

Row 4: Rep Row 2.
Rows 5–18: Rep Rows 1–2 seven times.
Row 19: Rep Row 1.

Row 20: Sl 1, p1, m1Rp, [purl to m, sm, work Raglan Lace, sm] 4 times, purl to last 2 sts, m1Lp, p1, k1. 2 neck sts inc'd.

Row 21: Sl 1, k1, m1L, [knit to 2 sts before m, ssk, yo, sm, work Raglan Lace, sm, yo, k2tog] 4 times, knit to last 2 sts, m1R, k2. 2 neck sts inc'd.

Row 22: Rep Row 20.
Row 23: Rep Row 1.
Row 24: Rep Row 20.

448 (466) sts: 54 (56) each front, 132 (138) in back, 92 (96) each sleeve, and 4 Raglan Lace sections of 6 sts each.

Round Yoke Section:
Size XS only:
Rnd 1 (RS): Sl 1, k1, m1L, [knit to m, yo, sm, work Raglan Lace, sm, yo] 4 times, knit to last 2 sts, m1R, k2. Do not turn. Use the backward loop method to CO 6 sts, pm and join to work in the round. 280 sts: 70 each front and back, 58 each sleeve, and 4 Raglan Lace sections of 6 sts each.

Rnd 2: [Knit to m, sm, work Raglan Lace, sm] 4 times, knit to end.

Rnd 3: [Knit to m, yo, sm, work Raglan Lace, sm, yo] 4 times, knit to end. 8 raglan sts inc'd.
Rnd 4: Rep Rnd 2.

Rnd 5: [Knit to 2 sts before m, ssk, yo, sm, work Raglan Lace, sm, yo, k2tog] 4 times, knit to end.
Rnd 6: Rep Rnd 2.
Rep Rnds 3–6 once more, then rep Rnds 3–4 once.

304 sts: 76 each front and back, 64 each sleeve, and 4 Raglan Lace sections of 6 sts each.

Size S only:
Rnd 1 (RS): Sl 1, k1, m1L, [knit to 2 sts before m, ssk, yo, sm, work Raglan Lace, sm, yo, k2tog] 4 times, knit to last 2 sts, m1R, k2. Do not turn. Use the backward loop method to CO 10 sts, pm and join to work in the round. 308 sts: 80 each front and back, 62 each sleeve, and 4 Raglan Lace sections of 6 sts each.

Rnd 2: [Knit to m, sm, work Raglan Lace, sm] 4 times, knit to end.
Rnd 3: [Knit to m, yo, ssk, work Raglan Lace, sm, yo] 4 times, knit to end. 8 raglan sts inc'd.
Rnd 4: Rep Rnd 2.

Rnd 5: [Knit to 2 sts before m, ssk, yo, sm, work Raglan Lace, sm, yo, k2tog] 4 times, knit to end.

Rnd 6: Rep Rnd 2.
Rnds 7–14: Rep Rnds 3–6 two times.
Rnds 15–18: Rep Rnds 5–6 two times.

332 sts: 86 each front and back, 68 each sleeve, and 4 Raglan Lace sections of 6 sts each.

Sizes – (–, M, L, XL, 2X, 3X, 4X) only:
Rnd 1 (RS): Sl 1, k1, m1L, [knit to 2 sts before m, ssk, yo, sm, work Raglan Lace, sm, yo, k2tog] 4 times, knit to last 2 sts, m1R, k2. Do not turn. Use the backward loop method to CO – (–, 14, 18, 18, 18, 22, 24) sts, pm and join to work in the round. – (–, 332, 372, 392, 432, 472, 492) sts: – (–, 88, 100, 106, 118, 132, 138) each front and back, – (–, 66, 74, 78, 86, 92, 96) each sleeve, and 4 Raglan Lace sections of 6 sts each.
Rnd 2: [Knit to m, sm, work Raglan Lace, sm] 4 times, knit to end.

Rnd 3: [Knit to m, yo, sm, work Raglan Lace, sm, yo] 4 times, knit to end.
8 raglan sts inc'd.
Rnd 4: Rep Rnd 2.

Rnd 5: [Knit to 2 sts before m, ssk, yo, sm, work Raglan Lace, sm, yo, k2tog] 4 times, knit to end.
Rnd 6: Rep Rnd 2.
Rep Rnds 3–6 – (–, 2, 2, 1, 1, 2, 2) more time(s), then rep Rnds 3–4 once.

– (–, 364, 404, 416, 456, 504, 524) sts: – (–, 96, 108, 112, 124, 140, 146) each front and back, – (–, 74, 82, 84, 92, 100, 104) each sleeve, and 4 Raglan Lace sections of 6 sts each.

Divide Body and Sleeves:
Rnd 1: [Knit to 2 sts before m, ssk, yo, sm, work Raglan Lace, sm, place next 64 (68, 74, 82, 84, 92, 100, 104) sts on holder for sleeve, use the backward loop method to CO 18 (18, 24, 24, 30, 30, 30, 36) sts for underarm, sm, work Raglan Lace, sm, yo, k2tog] 2 times, knit to end. 212 (232, 264, 288, 308, 332, 364, 388) body sts rem on needle.

Rnd 2: [Knit to m, sm, work Raglan Lace, sm] 4 times, knit to end.
Rnd 3: [Knit to 2 sts before m, ssk, yo, sm, work Raglan Lace, sm, yo, k2tog] 4 times, knit to end.
Rep Rnds 2–3 twice more, then rep Rnd 2 once more.

Set-up rnd: [Knit to m, sm, k6, remove m, knit to next m, remove m, k6, sm] 2 times, knit to end, remove beg-of-rnd m, knit to next m; this is beg of rnd from now on.

Knit all sts until body measures 2" / 5cm from underarm CO.

Dec Rnd: [Ssk, knit to 2 sts before m, k2tog, sm, knit to next m, sm] 2 times. 4 sts dec'd.

Rep Dec Rnd on every 6th rnd 8 (10, 9, 3, 4, 1, 1, 1) more times, then every 5th rnd 3 (1, 2, 7, 7, 7, 2, 0) times, then every 4th rnd 0 (0, 0, 1, 0, 3, 8, 10) times. 164 (184, 216, 240, 260, 284, 316, 340) sts.

Work even until body measures 10.75 (11, 10.75, 10, 10.25, 9.75, 9, 8.75)" / 27.5 (28, 27.5, 25.5, 26, 25, 23, 22)cm from underarm.

Inc Rnd: [K1, m1L, knit to 1 st before m, m1R, k1, sm, knit to next m, sm] 2 times. 4 sts inc'd.

Rep Inc Rnd on every 3rd rnd 9 more times, then every 4th rnd 8 times. 236 (256, 288, 312, 332, 356, 388, 412) sts.

Work even until body measures 17.75 (18, 17.75, 17, 17.25, 16.75, 16, 15.75)" / 45 (45.5, 45, 43, 44, 42.5, 40.5, 40)cm from underarm.

Next rnd: K15 (15, 18, 18, 21, 21, 21, 24), pm for new beg of rnd, knit to end removing all other m.
Next rnd: Knit, inc 30 (32, 36, 40, 42, 44, 48, 52) sts evenly spaced, working all incs as m1L. 266 (288, 324, 352, 374, 400, 436, 464) sts.

Work even until body measures 19.75 (20, 19.75, 19, 19.25, 18.75, 18, 17.75)" / 50 (51, 50, 48.5, 49, 47.5, 45.5, 45)cm from underarm.

BO as foll: K2, *insert left needle into 2 sts on right needle and k2tog, k1; rep from * to end, insert left needle into 2 sts on right needle and k2tog. Do not fasten off. Transfer rem st to crochet hook. With RS facing, work 1 sc into each bound-off st around. Join with sl st in first sc. Fasten off.

SLEEVES

Beg at center of underarm CO with dpns or long circular needle, pick up and knit 9 (9, 12, 12, 15, 15, 15, 18) sts from CO edge, pick up and knit tbl 2 sts in corner between CO sts and sts on holder, k1 from holder, pm, knit to last st on holder, pm, k1, pick up and knit tbl 2 sts in corner, pick up and knit 9 (9, 12, 12, 15, 15, 15, 18) sts from CO edge, pm for beg of rnd. 86 (90, 102, 110, 118, 126, 134, 144) sts.

Next rnd: Knit to 3 sts before m, k3tog, remove m, knit to m, remove m, sssk, knit to end. 82 (86, 98, 106, 114, 122, 130, 140) sts.
Knit 2 rnds.

Dec Rnd: K3, ssk, knit to last 5 sts, k2tog, knit to end. 2 sts dec'd.
Rep Dec Rnd on every 11th rnd 4 (2, 0, 0, 0, 0, 0, 0) more times, then every 9th rnd 4 (5, 3, 2, 0, 0, 0, 0) times, then every 7th rnd 5 (6, 9, 9, 10, 8, 9, 8) times, then every 5th rnd 4 (5, 9, 9, 10, 8, 9, 7) times, then every 3rd rnd 0 (0, 0, 3, 7, 10, 12, 16) times. 46 (48, 54, 58, 60, 64, 70, 76) sts.

Work even until sleeve measures 17 (17, 17.5, 17.5, 18, 18, 18.5, 18.5)" / 43 (43, 44.5, 44.5, 45.5, 45.5, 47, 47)cm from underarm.

Next rnd: Knit, inc 12 (12, 14, 16, 16, 16, 18, 20) sts evenly spaced, working all incs as m1L. 58 (60, 68, 74, 76, 80, 88, 96) sts.

Work even until sleeve measures 19 (19, 19.5, 19.5, 20, 20, 20.5, 20.5)" / 48.5 (48.5, 49.5, 49.5, 51, 51, 52, 52)cm from underarm.

BO and work single crochet edging as for body.

FINISHING

With WS of collar facing, beg where BO edge of collar meets neckline, use crochet hook to draw up a loop in edge of collar, ch 1, then work 1 sc in each st around edge of collar and neckline. Fasten off.

Weave in ends. Wet block.

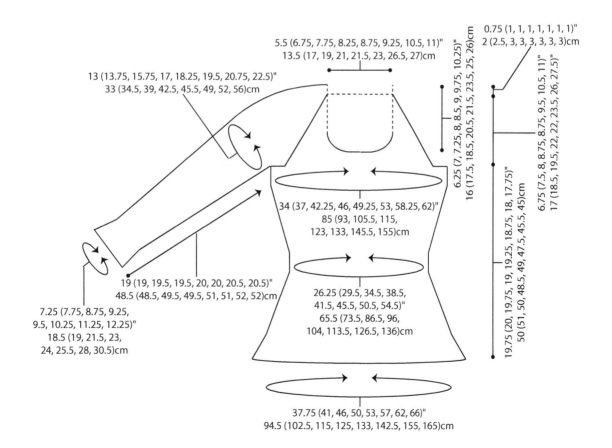

5.5 (6.75, 7.75, 8.25, 8.75, 9.25, 10.5, 11)"
13.5 (17, 19, 21, 21.5, 23, 26.5, 27)cm

13 (13.75, 15.75, 17, 18.25, 19.5, 20.75, 22.5)"
33 (34.5, 39, 42.5, 45.5, 49, 52, 56)cm

0.75 (1, 1, 1, 1, 1, 1, 1)"
2 (2.5, 3, 3, 3, 3, 3, 3)cm

6.25 (7, 7.25, 8, 8.5, 9, 9.75, 10.25)"
16 (17.5, 18.5, 20.5, 21.5, 23.5, 25, 26)cm

6.75 (7.5, 8, 8.75, 9.5, 10.5, 11)"
17 (18.5, 19.5, 22, 23.5, 26, 27.5)cm

34 (37, 42.25, 46, 49.25, 53, 58.25, 62)"
85 (93, 105.5, 115, 123, 133, 145.5, 155)cm

19 (19, 19.5, 19.5, 20, 20, 20.5, 20.5)"
48.5 (48.5, 49.5, 49.5, 51, 51, 52, 52)cm

26.25 (29.5, 34.5, 38.5, 41.5, 45.5, 50.5, 54.5)"
65.5 (73.5, 86.5, 96, 104, 113.5, 126.5, 136)cm

19.75 (20, 19.75, 19, 19.25, 18.75, 18, 17.75)"
50 (51, 50, 48.5, 49, 47.5, 45.5, 45)cm

7.25 (7.75, 8.75, 9.25, 9.5, 10.25, 11.25, 12.25)"
18.5 (19, 21.5, 23, 24, 25.5, 28, 30.5)cm

37.75 (41, 46, 50, 53, 57, 62, 66)"
94.5 (102.5, 115, 125, 133, 142.5, 155, 165)cm

SUTURE

Alexandra Tinsley

This curious hat uses an unusual slipped-stitch-pick-up technique to create ruching and a strange "stitched-up" effect. Very zombie chic... or, if you haven't been infected yet, pretty good camouflage.

PATTERN NOTES

The ruching and vertical "towers" on this hat are created by slipping stitches while knitting and leaving a float of yarn on the front of the work. Later, the floats are picked up with a crochet hook in the same manner as you would pick up a dropped stitch, a technique we call here "climbing the ladder."

STITCHES AND TECHNIQUES

CLIMBING THE LADDER

Working from RS of hat, insert crochet hook underneath bottom rung of ladder created by the slipped stitches, with hook facing forward. Snag second-to-bottom rung with hook and pull it underneath bottom-most rung. Now you have a loop on your hook. Insert hook under third-from-bottom rung, snag it, and pull through loop on the needle to create a new loop. Do the same with fourth-from-bottom rung, and so on, until you have climbed the ladder to the top. Now, snag the next stitch on the left knitting needle with hook, draw it through loop on hook, and place it back on left needle, ready to be worked.

PATTERN

With circular needle, CO 96 sts, pm, and join in the round, being careful not to twist.
Work [k1, p1] rib for 3.5" / 9cm. For a slouchier fit, knit longer before starting the ruching.

Rnd 1: Knit.
Rnd 2: [Sl 5 pwise wyif, k7] to end.
Rnds 3–40: Rep Rnds 1–2 nineteen times.

CROWN DECREASES

Change to dpns when necessary.
Rnd 41: K7, [s2pk, k9] 7 times, s2pk, k2. 80 sts.
Rnd 42: [Sl 5 wyif, k5] to end.
Rnd 43: K1, [s2pk, k7] 7 times, s2pk, k6. 64 sts.
Rnd 44: [Sl 3 wyif, k5] to end.
Rnd 45: K4, [s2pk, k5] 7 times, s2pk, k1. 48 sts.
Rnd 46: [Sl 1 wyif, k3] to end.
Rnd 47: [S2pk, k3] to end. 32 sts.
Rnd 48: [Climb the ladder (see Stitches and Techniques), k4] to end.
Rnd 49: [K1, s2pk] to end. 16 sts.
Rnd 50: [K2tog] to end. 8 sts.

FINISHING

Cut yarn leaving a long tail and draw through rem sts on needle. Pull snug and weave in all ends. Block gently.

SIZE

One size

Fits heads from 20–22" / 51–56cm comfortably

FINISHED MEASUREMENTS

Circumference: unstretched, 16" / 40.5cm; stretched, 22" / 56cm

MATERIALS

Madelinetosh tosh merino (100% superwash merino; 210 yds / 192m per 3.5oz skein); color: Glazed Pecan; 1 skein

16-inch US #7 / 4.5mm circular needle or size needed to obtain gauge
Set of US #7 / 4.5mm dpns or size needed to obtain gauge

US size H / 5mm crochet hook (or similar size)

Stitch marker, yarn needle

GAUGE

16 sts and 28 rows = 4" / 10 cm in St st

BULLETPROOF

Alexandra Virgiel

Okay, no, it won't actually stop bullets, but the sentiment is there and you shouldn't underestimate the power of a good "not-to-be-messed-with" vibe.

PATTERN NOTES

Yarn is held double throughout.

Vest is knit in the round to the armholes, then back and front are worked flat. Back straps wrap over the shoulder to the front, are shaped with short rows, and fastened with separating zippers.

You can order the zippers cut and finished to the correct length from zipperstop.com. Tip: Check whether a coordinating zipper is available before settling on a yarn color.

STITCHES AND TECHNIQUES

1X1 TWISTED RIB

(Worked in the round, even number of sts):
Rnd 1: [K1 tbl, p1 tbl] to end.
Rep Rnd 1.

(Worked flat, mult of 2 sts + 1):
Row 1: [K1 tbl, p1 tbl] to last st, k1 tbl.
Row 2: [P1 tbl, k1 tbl] to last st, p1 tbl.
Rep Rows 1–2.

PATTERN

BODY

With two strands of yarn held tog, CO 148 (160, 176, 188, 204, 216, 232) sts, pm and join to work in the round. Work in 1x1 Twisted Rib for 1.25" / 3cm.

Next rnd: Work 9 (9, 11, 11, 13, 13, 15) sts in rib, pm, k55 (61, 65, 71, 75, 81, 85), pm, work 19 (19, 23, 23, 27, 27, 31) sts in rib, pm, k55 (61, 65, 71, 75, 81, 85), pm, work 10 (10, 12, 12, 14, 14, 16) sts in rib.

Work in St st with rib panels as est until body measures 13.5 (13.5, 14, 14, 14.5, 14.5, 15)" / 34.5 (34.5, 35.5, 35.5, 37, 37, 38)cm from CO.

Divide back and front:
Work in rib to first m, sm, knit to second m, sm, work 5 sts in rib, BO 9 (9, 13, 13, 17, 17, 21) sts, work in rib to third m, sm, knit to fourth m, sm, work 5 sts in rib, place last 65 (71, 75, 81, 85, 91, 95) sts on a holder for back, BO 9 (9, 13, 13, 17, 17, 21) sts removing beg-of-rnd m. 65 (71, 75, 81, 85, 91, 95) sts rem on needle for front.

FRONT

Dec Row (RS): K1, work 4 sts in rib, sm, ssk, knit to 2 sts before m, k2tog, sm, work 4 sts in rib, k1. 2 sts dec'd.
Next row (WS): P1, work 4 sts in rib, sm, purl to m, sm, work 4 sts in rib, p1.
Rep the last 2 rows 7 (8, 9, 10, 10, 11, 11) more times. 49 (53, 55, 59, 63, 67, 71) sts.

Work even, maintaining 5-st borders at each edge, until front measures 3 (3.25, 3.5, 3.75, 4, 4.5, 4.75)" / 7.5 (8.5, 9, 9.5, 10, 11.5, 12)cm from underarm BO, ending with a WS row.

Work edging:
Row 1 (RS): K1, work twisted rib to last st, k1.
Row 2 (WS): P1, work twisted rib to last st, p1.
Row 3: Rep Row 1.
BO all sts in patt.

SIZES

Women's S (M, L, XL, 2X, 3X, 4X); shown in size S

Intended to be worn with at least 2" / 5cm of negative ease

FINISHED MEASUREMENTS

Bust: 30.75 (33.5, 36.5, 39.25, 42.25, 45, 48)" / 77 (83.5, 91.5, 98, 106, 112.5, 120.5)cm

MATERIALS

Berroco Comfort DK Solids (50% acrylic, 50% nylon; 178 yds / 163m per 50g ball); color: 2713 Dusk; 5 (6, 7, 7, 8, 8, 9) balls

24-inch US #9 / 5.5mm circular needle, or size needed to obtain gauge

Stitch markers, yarn needle, stitch holder or waste yarn, sewing needle and matching thread

Two 3.5 (4, 4, 4, 4.5, 4.5, 5)" / 9 (10, 10, 10, 11.5, 11.5, 12.5)cm #5 separating zippers

GAUGE

18 sts and 24 rows = 4" / 10cm in St st with yarn doubled

24 sts and 24 rows = 4" / 10cm in 1x1 Twisted Rib with yarn doubled

BACK

Replace 65 (71, 75, 81, 85, 91, 95) held sts on needle and join yarn with RS facing.

Dec Row (RS): K1, work 4 sts in rib, sm, ssk, knit to 2 sts before m, k2tog, sm, work 4 sts in rib, k1. 2 sts dec'd.
Next row (WS): P1, work 4 sts in rib, sm, purl to m, sm, work 4 sts in rib, p1.
Rep the last 2 rows 5 (6, 7, 8, 8, 9, 9) more times. 53 (57, 59, 63, 67, 71, 75) sts.

Work even, maintaining 5-st borders at each edge, until back measures 6 (6.25, 6.5, 6.75, 7, 7.5, 7.75)" / 15 (16, 16.5, 17, 18, 19, 19.5)cm from underarm BO, ending with a RS row.

Shape neck:
Row 1 (RS): K1, work 4 sts in rib, sm, k7 (9, 9, 9, 11, 11, 13), pm, work 29 (29, 31, 35, 35, 39, 39) sts in twisted rib, pm, k7 (9, 9, 9, 11, 11, 13), sm, work 4 sts in rib, k1.

Row 2 (WS): P1, work 4 sts in rib, sm, purl to m, sm, work in rib to m, sm, purl to m, sm, work 4 sts in rib, p1.

Row 3: Work even in est patt.

Row 4: P1, work 4 sts in rib, sm, purl to m, sm, work 5 sts in rib, BO 19 (19, 21, 25, 25, 29, 29) sts in patt, work 5 sts in rib, sm, purl to m, sm, work 4 sts in rib, p1. 17 (19, 19, 19, 21, 21, 23) sts rem each side.

Working on right shoulder only:
Dec Row (RS): K1, work 4 sts in rib, sm, knit to 2 sts before m, k2tog, sm, work 4 sts in rib, k1. 1 st dec'd.
Next row (WS): P1, work 4 sts in rib, sm, purl to m, sm, work 4 sts in rib, p1.
Rep the last 2 rows once more. 15 (17, 17, 17, 19, 19, 21) sts.

Work 6 rows even.

Inc Row (RS): K1, work 4 sts in rib, sm, knit to 1 st before m, RLI, k1, sm, work 4 sts in rib, k1. 1 st inc'd.
Rep Inc Row on every 4th row 3 more times. 19 (21, 21, 21, 23, 23, 25) sts.

Short row shaping:
Row 1 (WS): Work in patt to last 5 (6, 6, 6, 6, 6, 5) sts, w&t.
Row 2 (RS): Work in patt to end.

Row 3: Work in patt to 3 (3, 3, 3, 4, 4, 5) sts before previous wrapped st, w&t.
Row 4: Work in patt to end.

Rep Rows 3–4 twice more.

Next row (WS): Work in patt to end, picking up and purling wraps tog with wrapped sts.

Work edging:
Row 1 (RS): K1, work twisted rib to last st, k1.
Row 2 (WS): P1, work twisted rib to last st, p1.
Row 3: Rep Row 1.
BO all sts.

Left shoulder:
Return to left shoulder sts and join yarn with RS facing.
Dec Row (RS): K1, work 4 sts in rib, sm, ssk, knit to m, sm, work 4 sts in rib, k1. 1 st dec'd.
Next row (WS): P1, work 4 sts in rib, sm, purl to m, sm, work 4 sts in rib, p1.
Rep the last 2 rows once more. 15 (17, 17, 17, 19, 19, 21) sts.

Work 6 rows even.
Inc Row (RS): K1, work 4 sts in rib, sm, k1, LLI, knit to m, sm, work 4 sts in rib, k1. 1 st inc'd.
Rep Inc Row on every 4th row 3 more times. 19 (21, 21, 21, 23, 23, 25) sts.

Work 1 WS row even.

Short row shaping:
Row 1 (RS): Work in patt to last 5 (6, 6, 6, 6, 6, 5) sts, w&t.
Row 2 (WS): Work in patt to end.

Row 3: Work in patt to 3 (3, 3, 3, 4, 4, 5) sts before previous wrapped st, w&t.
Row 4: Work in patt to end.
Rep Rows 3–4 twice more.

Next row (RS): Work in patt to end, picking up and knitting wraps tog with wrapped sts.

Work edging:
Row 1 (WS): P1, work twisted rib to last st, p1.
Row 2 (RS): K1, work twisted rib to last st, k1.
Row 3: Rep Row 1.
BO all sts.

FINISHING

Wet block. Lightly steam shoulder straps to make them lie flat. Weave in ends. Sew in zippers.

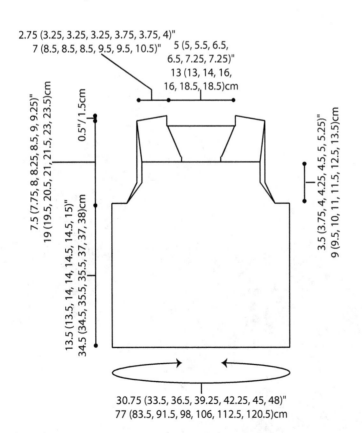

2.75 (3.25, 3.25, 3.25, 3.75, 3.75, 4)"
7 (8.5, 8.5, 8.5, 9.5, 9.5, 10.5)"

5 (5, 5.5, 6.5, 6.5, 7.25, 7.25)"
13 (13, 14, 16, 16, 18.5, 18.5)cm

0.5"/1.5cm

7.5 (7.75, 8, 8.25, 8.5, 9, 9.25)"
19 (19.5, 20.5, 21, 21.5, 23, 23.5)cm

13.5 (13.5, 14, 14, 14.5, 14.5, 15)"
34.5 (34.5, 35.5, 35.5, 37, 37, 38)cm

3.5 (3.75, 4, 4.25, 4.5, 5, 5.25)"
9 (9.5, 10, 11, 11.5, 12.5, 13.5)cm

30.75 (33.5, 36.5, 39.25, 42.25, 45, 48)"
77 (83.5, 91.5, 98, 106, 112.5, 120.5)cm

APOCKETMITTS

Flossie Arend

These unisex, camouflage-colored mitts are not just an accessory but also a survival tool. Two "secret" inner pockets (3" and 4.5" respectively) blend in almost seamlessly on the underside of mitts and are perfect for storing water purification and anti-radiation tablets, weaponry, compass, matches, or even a small phone. Inconspicuous snaps are sewn into the pockets to ensure nothing falls out. The mitts are interchangeable, and can be worn with pockets facing outwards or inwards. They are perfect for the scavenger on the go—never leave hovel without them!

PATTERN NOTES

Arm warmers begin with a provisional cast on at the wrist, then are worked upward to the elbow. The pockets are worked separately on a spare pair of needles, then knit into the arm warmers. The provisional cast on stitches are then placed back on the needles for the fingerless mitts portion. This construction allows the knitter to try on the mitts in stages to ensure perfect fit and length, and also gives the option to just make forearm sleeves (with a regular cast on) if so desired.

Both left and right arm warmers are worked almost identically. Only the pockets, thumbs, and rejoining for the fingerless mitts are different.

PATTERN: LEFT ARM WARMER

WRIST

With MC, provisionally CO 28 (32) sts. Pm and join to work in the round. Work in St st for 4" / 10cm.
Next round: K1, m1L, k12 (14), m1R, k2, m1L, k12 (14), m1R, k1. 32 (36) sts. Set aside.

FIRST POCKET

With second set of needles and CC, CO 7 (8) sts and work in St st for 3" / 7.5cm, ending with a WS row. Cut CC.

Returning to original MC piece, use MC and k2, transfer next 7 (8) MC sts to waste yarn, knit across 7 (8) pocket sts, knit to end of rnd.

ARM

Rnds 1–6: Knit.
Rnd 7: K1, pm, m1L, k14 (16), m1R, pm, k2, pm, m1L, k14 (16), m1R, pm, k1. 36 (40) sts.
Rnds 8–13: Knit.
Rnd 14: K1, sm, m1L, knit to m, m1R, sm, knit to next m, sm, m1L, knit to m, m1R, sm, k1. 4 sts inc'd.
Rep Rnds 8–14 one (two) more time(s). 44 (52) sts.
Work even until piece measures 9.75" / 25cm from CO, or until arm warmer reaches from wrist to about 1.5" / 4cm short of elbow crease. Set aside.

Size M/L only:
Rnds 22–28: Rep Rows 8–14. 52 sts.

SIZES

S/M (M/L); shown in size S/M
Intended to be worn with 1–2" / 2.5–5cm of negative ease.

FINISHED MEASUREMENTS

Length: 14 (14.25)" / 35.5 (36)cm
Palm circumference: 6 (6.75)" / 15 (17)cm
Wrist circumference: 5.5 (6.5)" / 14 (16)cm
Forearm circumference: 8.75 (10.5)" / 22 (26)cm

MATERIALS

Madelinetosh tosh merino DK (100% superwash merino; 225 yds / 206m per 100g skein)

⚞ [MC] Badlands; 1 (2) skeins

⚞ [CC] Dustbowl; 1 skein (or 40 yds / 37m of DK-weight yarn)

32-inch US #7 / 4.5mm circular needle, pair of circular needles, or set of dpns as needed for your preferred method of working in the round, or size needed to obtain gauge

Extra pair/set of US #7 / 4.5mm needles for working pockets

Removable stitch markers, 10 size 1/0 sew-on snaps, waste yarn, yarn needle, sewing needle and thread

GAUGE

20 sts and 30 rnds = 4"/ 10 cm in St st

RECOMMENDED GAMING

Contributed by Flossie Arend unless otherwise indicated.

⚜ Fallout

Set in an apocalyptic future on an alternate post-World War II timeline, Fallout places the player as a survivor who must brave the wastelands in order to retrieve necessities for communities driven underground by nuclear "fallout." Beautifully rendered and lauded within the gamer community, Fallout has won numerous awards and continues to be one of the finest post-apocalyptic gaming experiences.

⚜ Half-Life 2

Critically acclaimed and beloved among gamers, Half-Life 2 occurs in a dystopic, alternate future where humans are mined as resources by alien overlords. The player must lead the resistance to free all of humanity.

⚜ Left 4 Dead/Left 4 Dead 2

Four survivors struggle through a ruined landscape that has been consumed by zombies. Equipped with hand-to-hand weapons and firearms, players team up online in sets of four to battle through different landscapes and eventually reach rescue.

⚜ The Walking Dead

Based loosely on both the TV show and the original comic book, this point-and-click, role-playing adventure game centers on a small, fluctuating group of survivors. The player must often choose who lives and who dies, with real stakes, measurable outcomes, and decision-making that inevitably changes gameplay.

⚜ Call of Duty: Black Ops Zombies

A subset of the CoD: Black Ops game, Black Ops Zombies pits four online players against a never-ending zombie onslaught. Weaponry must be paid for with points earned through kills, and levels get progressively harder with each round of play.

⚜ Darksiders/Darksiders II

The war between Heaven and Hell has finally erupted, and the Four Horsemen of the Apocalypse are asked to intervene and restore order. Within this turmoil, humanity and the Kingdom of Man is born. The player assumes the role of one of the Horsemen, War, as you battle to right a world gone awry.

⚜ Dead Rising 2

Set in the post-apocalypse, the player assumes the role of Chuck Greene, a motocross champion whose daughter Katey has been affected by the zombie virus and requires daily doses of Zombrex in order not to turn. To find more Zombrex, Chuck must fight his way through the landscape, building unlikely weaponry from supplies he finds. A number of endings are possible based upon the player's choices.

⚜ Deus Ex

A role-playing/ first-person shooter, Deus Ex takes place in a dystopic future ravaged by terrorist attacks in which several underground organizations are involved. The perfect game for conspiracy theorists, Deus Ex explores the possibility of aliens, biological warfare, fictional monsters, and more, and focuses on a society where the divide between rich and poor has widened severely.

⚜ Zombies, Run!

An iPhone app game that you play by actually running. From zombies. Can't hurt to get in shape and get some practice, you know.
—Alexandra Tinsley

Both sizes:
Knit for another 2.75 (2)" / 7 (5)cm, or until approximately 1.5"/ 4cm from elbow crease. Set aside.

SECOND POCKET

With second set of needles and CC, CO 13 (15) sts and work in St st for 4.5" / 11.5cm, ending with a WS row. Cut CC.

Returning to original MC piece, use MC and k3, transfer next 13 (15) MC sts to waste yarn, knit across 13 (15) pocket sts, knit to end of rnd.

UPPER FOREARM

Rnds 1–6: Knit.
Rnd 7: Purl.
Rnd 8: Knit.
Rnd 9: Purl.
BO all sts.

HAND

Carefully return 28 (32) provisional CO sts to needle(s).

With pocketless side of arm warmer (back of hand) facing you, join MC and pm for beg of rnd.
Rnds 1–3: Knit.
Rnd 4: [K7 (8), m1] 4 times. 32 (36) sts.

THUMB GUSSET SET-UP

Rnds 5–7: Knit.
Rnd 8: K1, m1L, pm for gusset, knit to last st, pm for gusset, m1R, k1. 34 (38) sts; 4 sts between gusset m.

Rnd 9: Knit.
Rnd 10: Knit to first gusset m, m1L, sm, knit to second gusset m, sm, m1R, knit to end. 2 sts inc'd.
Rep Rnds 9–10 three (four) more times. 42 (48) sts; 12 (14) sts between gusset m.

Knit 1 rnd.
Next rnd: Knit to first gusset m, place 6 (7) sts just worked on waste yarn for thumb, remove m, knit to second gusset m, remove m, place next 6 (7) sts on waste yarn for thumb. 30 (34) sts rem.

PALM

Rnds 1–11: Knit.
Rnd 12: Purl.
Rnd 13: Knit.

Rnd 14: Purl.
BO all sts.

LEFT THUMB

Return 12 (14) held sts to needle(s). With side of arm warmer with pockets facing you, k6 (7), pm, k6 (7), pick up and knit 2 sts from mitt, knit to m. 14 (16) sts.

Rnds 1–3: Knit.
Rnd 4: Purl.
Rnd 5: Knit.
Rnd 6: Purl.
BO all sts.

PATTERN: RIGHT ARM WARMER

Work Wrist as for Left Arm Warmer.

FIRST POCKET

With second set of needles and CC, CO 7 (8) sts and work in St st for 3" / 7.5cm, ending with a WS row. Cut CC.

Returning to original MC piece, use MC and k23 (26), transfer next 7 (8) MC sts to waste yarn, knit across 7 (8) pocket sts, k2.

Work Arm as for Left Arm Warmer.

SECOND POCKET

With second set of needles and CC, CO 13 (15) sts and work in St st for 4.5" / 11.5cm, ending with a WS row. Cut CC.

Returning to original MC piece, use MC and k28 (34), transfer next 13 (15) MC sts to waste yarn, knit 13 (15) pocket sts, k3.

Work Upper Forearm as for Left Arm Warmer.

RIGHT HAND

With sides of arm warmer with pockets (palm side) facing you, join MC and pm for beg of rnd. Work as for Left Arm Warmer.

RIGHT THUMB

Return 12 (14) sts to needles. With pocketless side of arm warmer facing you, k6 (7), pm, k6 (7), pick up and knit 2 sts from mitt, knit to m. 14 (16) sts.

Work as for Left Thumb.

FINISHING (BOTH MITTS)

Remove waste yarn from pocket sts and return to needles. With RS facing, join MC, leaving a 4" / 10 cm tail, and knit 1 row, purl 1 row. Measure out yarn 4 times the length of the pocket opening, and cut. BO using Elizabeth Zimmermann's Sewn Bind Off. The tails on either side of the pocket will be used to tack down the side edges and prevent them from curling.

Turn arm warmers inside out. Weave scrap yarn down the line of arm warmer sts that mark the edge of the pocket to create a sight line that is straight and easy to follow. Use MC to whip stitch pocket to arm warmer, skipping one row on both the pocket and the arm warmer for every st to further conceal the pockets on the right side. It is easiest and cleanest to connect the outer leg of the pocket sts to the tops (as opposed to the legs) of the arm warmer sts. Remove scrap yarn used as sight line.

Sew 2 snaps inside small pocket and 3 snaps inside large pocket, evenly spacing them across the lip of the pocket and as close to the top edge as possible to keep the pocket flap flat.

Weave in all ends, and close up any gaps between thumb and hand. Block using desired method.

RECOMMENDED READING

⚇ *Cloud Atlas* by David Mitchell

Described as a "puzzle novel," this fascinating book consists of six nested stories that take the reader from the 1800's to a post-apocalyptic future. The stories intertwine in surprising and fascinating ways as the book spirits you through time and space—but, alas, the opportunities for spoilers abound and I've already said too much! The 2012 film, while not strictly loyal to the book, is an entrancing and entertaining counterpart.

⚇ *Oryx and Crake* by Margaret Atwood

In the not-so-distant future where genetic engineering is commonplace (care for a delicious ChickieNob?), this story tells of the lives of a possibly warped genius, his unwitting friend, and a girl whom they may or may not have seen in internet porn as they either destroy or save society.

⚇ The *Hunger Games* series by Suzanne Collins

Just in case you've been living under a rock, the *Hunger Games* trilogy follows the story of a teenage girl named Katniss living in the dystopian Panem, which exists on the remains of North America. She finds herself playing in the Hunger Games, a yearly battle to the death that the elitist Capitol inflicts on the districts of Panem to remind them of a previous, failed

uprising. Meanwhile, there's some love triangle stuff going on. While the writing is distinctly "Young Adult"-ish, these books are still an enjoyable read that will leave you feeling paranoid and, if you're anything like me, constantly plotting the deaths of those around you. The movie does not, in this reviewer's opinion, live up to the books.

⚇ *Alas, Babylon* by Pat Frank

Published in the midst of cold war hysteria, this is the story of the nuclear war that almost was. *Alas, Babylon* follows a group of survivors in rural Florida as they struggle to get by after the Russians attack. The chilling realism of this book will shake you to your core, and leave you painfully aware of just how unprepared you are for disaster (unless, of course, you are way, way more prepared than the average person). The urge to move to the wilderness and learn to be self-sufficient immediately is to be expected.

⚇ *On the Beach* by Nevil Shute

The rest of the world destroyed as a result of nuclear warfare, the last remaining survivors in Australia wait for the fall out to reach them as well. What do you do when the world is over and you only have a few weeks to live? (Warning: the movie version has some

great old-timey eye candy—helllooo, Gregory Peck—but there is an awful lot of Waltzing Matilda and stiff acting.)

⚇ *Parable of the Sower* by Octavia E. Butler

Climate change and social ills (and particularly a drug called "pyro" that turns arson into an erotically ecstatic experience) have eroded American society, though some basic infrastructure struggles on. In the chaotic remains of southern California, an unusual girl loses her family and security. She must rebuild both among the other survivors, while searching for a better place and a better life.

⚇ *Dhalgren* by Samuel R. Delaney

Bellona, a US Midwestern city, is, for unexplained reasons, cut off from the rest of the world. A perpetual cloud covers the city, and there are two moons. And in this city set apart, a man who cannot remember his name and two friends explore the city, sanity, sexuality, love, and violence; often while dressed in holograms. There's also a novel within a novel, offering opportunity to re-arrange how you read: novel one, novel two, or page by page. —*Rebecca Zicarelli*

For more reading recommendations, see page 155.

EPILOGUE:
RISING FROM THE ASHES

Good job, you survived the worst of it. But who will you be in the grisly world of tomorrow?

Situation: The immediate danger has passed and the situation has stabilized. Survivors are left to rebuild society and find their roles going forward. Lawlessness and chaos still reign, but some semblance of order may begin to emerge among the more civilized set. But some survivors will eschew all trappings of Pre-Fall life, preferring to revert to a hunter-gatherer lifestyle. Still others might say, "Huh, I bet this old spaceship still works..."

Dystopian Dandies

The Dandies! The upper crust, the top o' the muffin, the cream that rises to the top of the barrel of toxic sludge. Some people will take any opportunity to get ahead, and reassembling a shattered society with yourself at the top is one way to do it! But you can't be too angry—at least someone is picking up the pieces, and their shabby dominion is nothing to write home about anyway.

Lunar Progression

Theressa Silver

After civilization falls and Monday morning staff meetings are a thing of the past, survivors will still need a way to keep track of the passage of time. Lunar Progression is a large cozy scarf/stole with a built in lunar calendar! At one end is a circle set into a diamond with buttons at the four corners that mark the four quarters of the lunar cycle. The pointer moves freely on its button pivot point. A button is moved along the length of the pointer to tick off the seven days of each quarter. On the other end of the scarf is another circle with a pointer and 13 buttons around its perimeter to mark the 13 lunar cycles in a year. The main body of the scarf has a lace ribbing pattern and tapers slightly from the diamond end to the circle end. There is a slit at the top point of the diamond that allows the other end to be threaded through to secure the scarf around the wearer.

PATTERN NOTES

BUTTONS

Buttons play a key role on this scarf. The two screw-head buttons pictured here were a lucky vintage find. If you cannot find screw heads, plain domed buttons will look like rivets. The buttons used for the waxing and waning half moons are Dill-Buttons #1048. In total you will need:

- Thirteen ½" / 13mm plain buttons
- One ½" / 13mm inch plain button (can be the same as other 13 or different)

- Two ½" / 13mm screw head or rivet-looking buttons
- One ¾" / 19mm all dark button
- One ¾" / 19mm all light button
- Two ¾" / 19mm half dark, half light buttons

STITCHES AND TECHNIQUES

LATTICE STITCH

(Worked flat, mult of 4 sts)
Row 1 (RS): [K2tog, yo, k2] to end.
Row 2 (WS): [P2tog, yo, p2] to end.
Rep Rows 1–2.

SEED STITCH

(Multiple of 2 sts)
Row/Rnd 1: [P1, k1] to end.
Row/Rnd 2: Knit the purl sts and purl the knit sts.
Rep Row/Rnd 2.

PATTERN

DIAMOND END CIRCLE

CO 8 sts onto one dpn.

Rnd 1: Starting with the first CO st and bringing the working yarn across the back as if for an i-cord, knit 2 sts onto

SIZES

Short (Long, Extra Long); shown in Extra Long

FINISHED MEASUREMENTS

Length: 47 (80, 110)" / 119.5 (203, 279.5)cm

MATERIALS

Cephalopod Yarns Traveller (100% superwash merino; 280 yds / 256m per 113g skein); color: House of Strangers; 2 (3, 4) skeins

Set of five US #8 / 5mm dpns, or size needed to obtain gauge
24-inch US #8 / 5mm circular needle
US #6 / 4mm straight needles

Stitch markers, stitch holders, yarn needle, sewing needle and thread (to attach buttons), 20 buttons (see Pattern Notes)

GAUGE

18 sts and 30 rows = 4" / 10cm in St st, on larger needles

23 sts and 24 rows = 4" / 10cm in Lattice Stitch, on larger needles

Gauge is not crucial for this pattern, but working at a very different gauge may change the yarn requirement.

first dpn, knit next 2 sts onto second dpn, and so on until you have 2 sts each on four needles.

Rnd 2: [M1, k1, m1, k1] 4 times. 16 sts.
Rnd 3: [K2, pm, k2] 4 times.

Rnd 4: [M1, knit to m, sm, m1, knit to end of needle] 4 times. 8 sts inc'd.
Rnd 5: Knit.
Rep Rnds 4–5 twelve more times. 120 sts.
Next rnd: Purl, removing m as you go.

TRANSITION TO DIAMOND

This section "boxes the circle" by short-rowing four corners onto the circle, working over one 30-st section at a time.

Row 1 (RS): K28, w&t.
Row 2 (WS): P26, w&t.

Row 3: Knit to 2 sts before previous wrapped st, w&t.
Row 4: Purl to 2 sts before previous wrapped st, w&t.

Rows 5–14: Rep Rows 3–4 five more times.

Row 15 (RS): K16, picking up and knitting wraps tog with wrapped sts as you go. Do not turn.
Rep Rows 1–15 three more times.

Change to circular needle and pm for beg of rnd.

Note: As you work the next rnd, pick up and work rem wraps tog with wrapped sts.
Next rnd: [P1, k1] 7 times, kfb, pm, kfb, *[p1, k1] 14 times, kfb, pm, kfb; rep from * 2 more times, [p1, k1] 7 times. 128 sts.

Next rnd: Work in seed st as est.
Inc Rnd: [Work in seed st to 1 st before m, kfb, sm, kfb] 4 times, work in seed st to end. 8 sts inc'd.
Rep the last 2 rnds twice more. 152 sts.

Next rnd (partial rnd): Work 19 sts in seed st, BO 76 sts. Do not turn. 76 sts rem.

TRANSITION TO SCARF BODY

With RS facing, place the second half of the sts on a holder for left side. You should have 38 sts left on the needle, ready to work a RS row, followed by 38 sts on a holder.

Note: As you work this section, work only the sts shown in the chart for each row, leaving unused sts on the needle and simply turning the work to start the next row (no wraps needed).

Beg with a RS row, work Rows 1–36 of Transition Chart 1 once, then rep Rows 35–36 for a further 6" / 15cm, ending with Row 35. Cut yarn and place these 38 sts on a holder for right side.

Return 38 held left side sts to needle and join yarn with WS facing.

Beg with a WS row, work Rows 1–36 of Transition Chart 2 once, then rep Rows 35–36 for a further 6" / 15cm, ending with Row 35. Do not turn work and do not cut yarn. Transfer 38 held right side sts to needle with WS facing and work Transition Chart 1, Row 36 across. 76 sts.

All sts are now on the needle and the two halves of the scarf are joined.

Next row (RS): [P1, k1] twice, p1, [k2tog, yo, k2] 7 times, [k1, p1] twice, k2tog, [p1, k1] twice, [k2tog, yo, k2] 7 times, [k1, p1] 2 times, k1. 75 sts.

Next row (WS): [K1, p1] twice, k1, [p2tog, yo, p2] 8 times, p3tog, yo, p2, [p2tog, yo, p2] 7 times, [p1, k1] twice, p1. 74 sts.

SCARF BODY

Work even in Lattice Stitch with first and last 5 sts in seed st for a further 0 (33, 63)" / 0 (84, 160)cm, ending with a WS row. Add or subtract rows here to adjust total length if desired.

Dec Row (RS): Work 4 sts in patt, p2tog, work to last 6 sts, k2tog, work in patt to end. 2 sts dec'd.

Rep Dec Row on every 12th row 11 more times. 50 sts. Work the partial Lattice Stitch repeats at the beginning and end of each row as detailed in Table 1.

TRANSITION TO CIRCLE END

Note: As you work this section, work only the sts shown in the chart for each row, leaving unused sts on the needle and simply turning the work to start the next row (no wraps needed).

Beginning with a WS row, work Rows 1–21 of Transition Chart 3. Do not turn at the end of the last row, but continue across the row working Row 1 of Transition Chart 4. Then work Rows 2–21 of chart 4.

TABLE 1

Number of sts available	At beginning of row, work:	At end of row, work:
3	(RS) K2tog, yo, k1	(RS) K2tog, yo, k1
	(WS) P2tog, yo, p1	(WS) P2tog, yo, p1
2	(RS) K2	(RS) K2tog, yo
	(WS) P2	(WS) P2tog, yo
1	(RS) K1	(RS) K1
	(WS) P1	(WS) P1

CIRCLE

With RS facing, use the cable method to CO 54 sts. 104 sts.
Row 1 (RS): [K8, pm] 13 times, join to work in the round.
Rnd 2: Purl.
Note: Change to dpns when necessary.
Rnd 3: [K2tog, knit to m, sm] 13 times. 91 sts.
Rnd 4: Purl.
Rnd 5: Knit.
Rnd 6: Purl.

Rnd 7: [K2tog, knit to m, sm] 13 times. 13 sts dec'd.
Rnds 8–9: Knit.
Rep Rnds 7–9 five more times. 13 sts.

Next rnd: [K1, k2tog] 4 times, k1. 9 sts. Cut the yarn leaving a long tail. With a tapestry needle, thread the tail through the rem sts, slipping them off the needle, and cinch closed.

7 DAY POINTER

With straight needles, CO 2 sts.
Row 1 (WS): Knit.
Row 2 (RS): [Kfb] twice. 4 sts.
Row 3: K1, p2, k1.
Row 4: K1, [kfb] twice, k1. 6 sts.
Row 5: K2, p2, k2.
Row 6: K1, p1, k2, p1, k1.

Row 7: K2, p1, yo, p1, k2. 7 sts.
Row 8: K1, p1, k3, p1, k1.
Row 9: K2, p3, k2.

Row 10: K1, p1, k3, pass first knit st over the foll two sts, p1, k1. 6 sts.
Rep Rows 7–10 eight more times.

Next row (RS): K2, p2, k2.
Next row: Ssk, [k2tog] twice. 3 sts.
Next row: Sl 2 as if to k2tog, k1, pass 2 slipped sts over, cut yarn and fasten off.

13 CYCLE POINTER

With straight needles, CO 2 sts.
Row 1 (WS): Knit.
Row 2 (RS): [Kfb] twice. 4 sts.
Row 3: Knit.
Row 4: K2, yo, k2. 5 sts.

Row 5: K1, p4.
Row 6: K3, p2.
Row 7: P1, k2, p2.
Row 8: K1, p2, k2.
Row 9: P3, k2.
Row 10: P1, k4.
Rep Rows 5–10 three more times.

Next row: K1, p2tog, yo, p2.
Next row: Ssk, k1, k2tog. 3 sts.
Knit 1 row.
Next row: Sl 2 as if to k2tog, k1, pass 2 slipped sts over, cut yarn and fasten off.

FINISHING

Weave in ends. Block.

Attach buttons and pointers using photo as a guide.

TRANSITION CHART 1

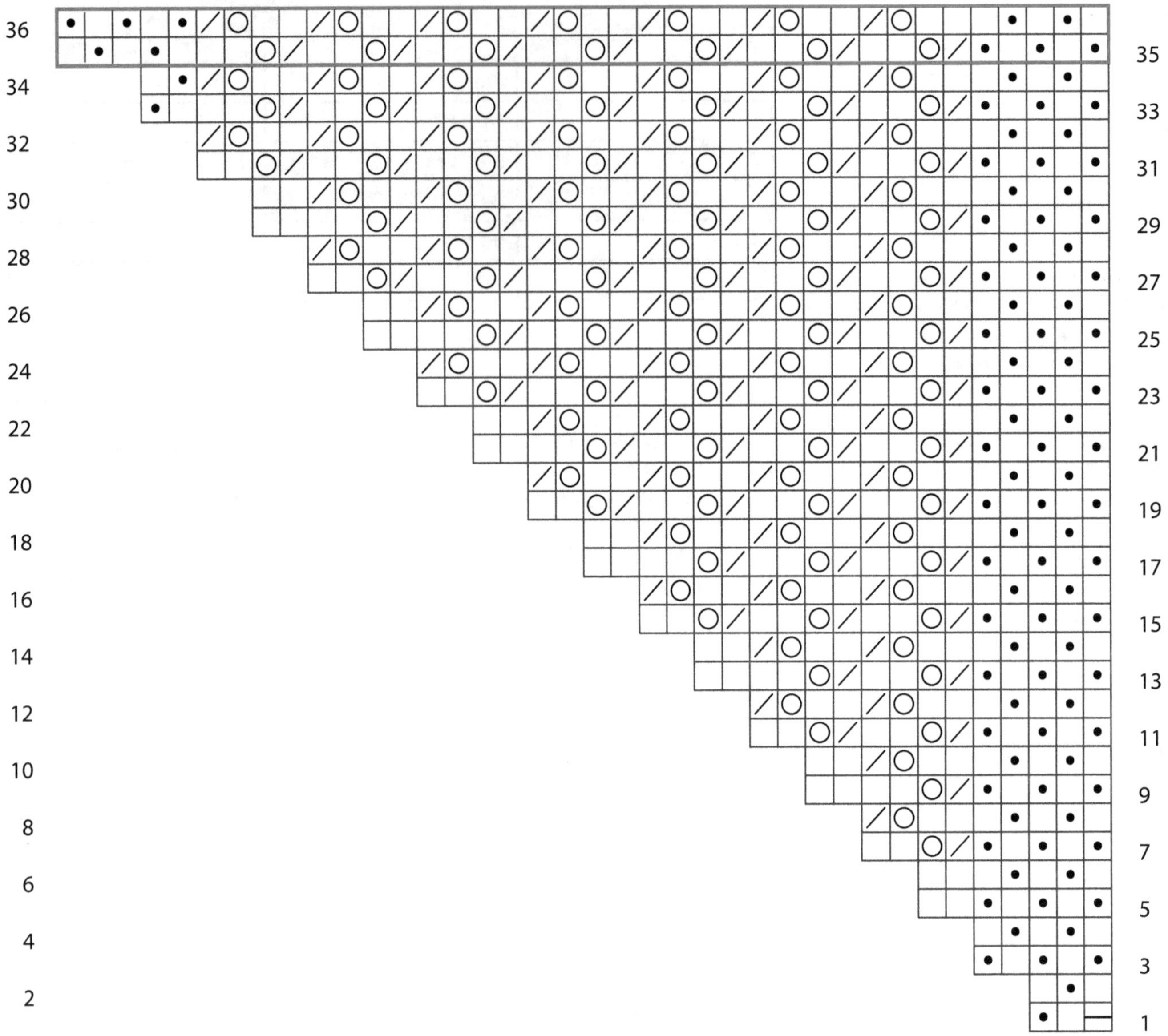

- □ RS: knit; WS: purl
- • RS: purl; WS: knit
- / RS: k2tog; WS: p2tog
- O yo
- V RS: sl 1 wyib; WS: sl1 wyif
- — st already on right needle after BO
- □ pattern repeat

TRANSITION CHART 2

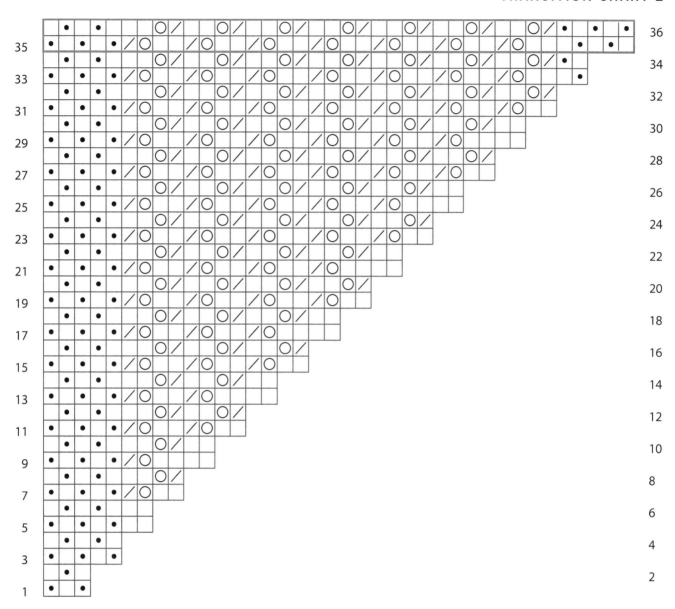

TRANSITION CHART 3

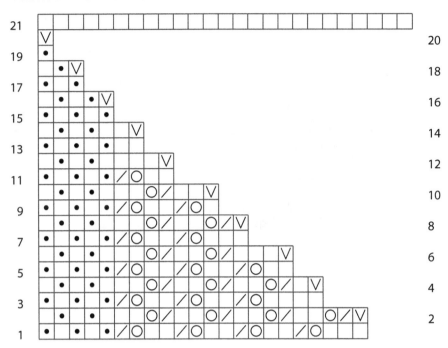

TRANSITION CHART 4

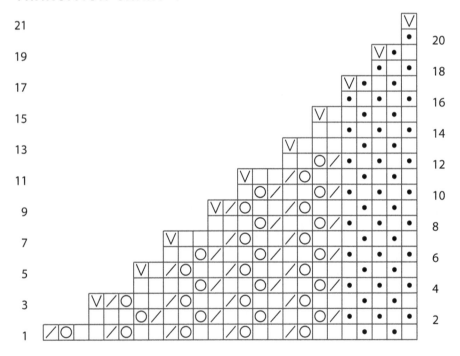

(Possible) Creatures of the Apocalypse and How to Fight Them

ZOMBIES

Killed by: Removing the head or destroying the brain.

Impeded by: Cunning

VAMPIRES

Killed by: Exposure to sunlight, wooden stake through the heart, burning, tearing off the head.

Impeded by: Silver (slows healing process), garlic, mirrors, tiny, countable objects such as grains of rice, holy water, crosses, Bibles, knotted rope or net, high pitched bells, romantic involvement with Slayers

EVIL ROBOTS AND/OR COMPUTERS

Killed by: Smelting, viruses, submersion, physical damage from guns or axes ... it depends on the machine.

ALIENS

Killed by: Sending Will Smith into the mother ship's belly, dandruff shampoo, a genius child cleverly blowing them all up, water, fire, Earth germs, the song "Indian Love Call" by Slim Whitman ... it kind of depends on the alien.

WEREWOLVES (HEY, YOU NEVER KNOW!)

Killed by: Silver to the heart (bullet, knife), regular human-type killing methods, but amplified.

Ringmaster

Rhiannon McCulloch

The world of the new elite is all bread and circuses, and every circus needs a ringmaster. This jacket, though detailed, is virtually seamless, with a timeless military flavor that is not accidental—though a ringmaster may seem dignified and perhaps even jovial, it would behoove you not to forget that they are the ones running the show.

PATTERN NOTES

The jacket peplum is knit first, from side to side in two halves which are joined with a decorative insert which is knit in the opposite direction. The peplum features a pocket on either side. The jacket body is picked up from the top edge of the Peplum and features a slightly lowered front waist. Slip stitches are used for decorative effect to replicate traditional darts. A facing is knit with the jacket and folds under to finish the jacket front neatly. The shoulders are worked with short rows and the sleeves are picked up from the armhole and worked using short rows. The collar is picked up from the neck edge and also shaped using short rows.

When you are working in stockinette and encounter a wrap from a previous short row, always pick up and work the wrap together with the wrapped st. In seed stitch, there is no need to pick up the wraps.

STITCHES AND TECHNIQUES

SEED STITCH

(Worked flat, mult of 2 sts)
Row 1 (WS): [K1, p1] to end.
Row 2 (RS): [P1, k1] to end.
Rep Rows 1–2.

(Worked flat, mult of 2 sts + 1)
Row 1: [K1, p1] to last st, k1.
Rep Row 1.

PATTERN

RIGHT PEPLUM

Front facing:
Using larger 32" circular needle, MC, and cable method, CO 60 (61, 62, 63, 64, 64, 65, 66, 66, 67) sts.

Knit 1 row. Purl 1 row.
Inc Row (RS): Knit to last 2 sts, kfb, k1. 1 st inc'd.

Cont in St st, rep Inc Row on every RS row 4 more times. 65 (66, 67, 68, 69, 69, 70, 71, 71, 72) sts.
Purl 1 WS row.
Next row (RS): Purl. (This creates a fold line for the front facing).

Peplum:
Purl 1 WS row.
Dec Row (RS): Knit to last 4 sts, k2tog, k2. 1 st dec'd.
Next row (WS): K2, purl to end.
Keeping 2 sts at edge in garter st throughout, rep Dec Row on every RS row 2 more times. 62 (63, 64, 65, 66, 66, 67, 68, 68, 69) sts.

Short Row (WS): K2, purl to last 5 sts, w&t.
Rep Dec Row on next row, then on foll 3 RS rows. Rep Short Row. Rep from * to * once more. 54 (55, 56, 57, 58, 58, 59, 60, 60, 61) sts.
Rep Dec Row on next row. 53 (54, 55, 56, 57, 57, 58, 59, 59, 60) sts.
Work 1 WS row even.

SIZES

To fit bust 30 (32, 34, 36, 38, 40, 42, 44, 46, 48)" / 76 (81, 86, 91.5, 96.5, 101.5, 106.5, 111.5, 117, 122)cm; shown in size to fit 34" / 86cm

FINISHED MEASUREMENTS

Bust: 33.5 (36.5, 38, 40.5, 42, 43.5, 46.5, 48, 51, 52.5)" / 84 (91, 95, 102, 105, 109, 116, 120, 127, 131)cm

Intended to be worn with 4" / 10cm of positive ease.

MATERIALS

[MC] Skeinz Vintage 8ply/DK (100% pure New Zealand wool; 114 yds/104m per 50g ball); color: Portwine; 15 (15, 17, 19, 20, 21, 22, 23, 24, 25) balls

[CC] Skeinz Merino Soft 4ply (100% merino wool; 195 yds / 175m yds per 50g ball); color: Black; 1 ball

32-inch and 16-inch US #6 / 4mm circular needles, or size needed to obtain gauge

Set of US #6 / 4mm dpns
32-inch US #3 / 3.25mm circular needle
US #3 / 3.25mm straight needles

Stitch markers, yarn needle, stitch holders or waste yarn, cable needle, sixteen ¾" / 19mm buttons

GAUGE

22 sts and 30 rows = 4" / 10cm in St st with MC, on larger needle

28 sts = 4" / 10cm in seed st with MC, on smaller needle

POCKET OPENING

Next row (RS): K15, turn.
Cont on these 15 sts only, work 31 rows even in St st, ending with a WS row. Place these 15 sts on a holder.

Rejoin yarn to rem 38 (39, 40, 41, 42, 42, 43, 44, 44, 45) sts.
Row 1 (RS): Knit to last 3 sts, sl 1, k2.
Row 2: K2, purl to end.
Row 3: Knit to last 4 sts, k2tog, k2. 37 (38, 39, 40, 41, 41, 42, 43, 43, 44) sts.
Row 4: Rep Row 2.
Row 5: Rep Row 1.
Row 6 (short row): K2, purl to last 2 sts, w&t.

Row 7: Knit to last 4 sts, k2tog, k2. 1 st dec'd.
Row 8: K2, purl to end.
Row 9: Knit to last 3 sts, sl 1, k2.
Row 10: Rep Row 8.
Row 11: Rep Row 7. 1 st dec'd.
Row 12: Rep Row 8.
Row 13: Knit to last 3 sts, sl 1, k2.
Row 14 (short row): K2, purl to last 2 sts, w&t.
Rep Rows 7–14 three more times, then Rows 7–9 once. 28 (29, 30, 31, 32, 32, 33, 34, 34, 35) sts.

Next row (WS): K2, purl to end, place 15 sts from holder on left needle with WS facing and purl across. 43 (44, 45, 46, 47, 47, 48, 49, 49, 50) sts.

Peplum continues:
Next row (RS): Knit to last 3 sts, sl 1, k2.
Short Row: K2, purl to last 5 sts, w&t.

Cont in St st, slipping the 3rd-to-last st on every RS row and keeping 2 sts at edge in garter st, rep Short Row every 8 rows 6 (7, 9, 10, 11, 12, 13, 14, 16, 17) more times.

Work even until shorter edge of peplum measures 13.75 (15.25, 16, 17.5, 18.25, 19, 20.5, 21.25, 22.5, 23.25)" / 35.5 (39, 41, 44.5, 46.5, 48, 52, 53.5, 57, 59) cm from facing fold line, ending with a RS row.

Next row (WS): Knit.
Place sts on holder. Cut yarn leaving a long tail for 3-needle BO.

LEFT PEPLUM

Front facing:
Using larger 32" circular needle, MC, and cable method, CO 60 (61, 62, 63, 64, 64, 65, 66, 66, 67) sts.

Knit 1 row. Purl 1 row.
Inc Row (RS): K1, kfb, knit to end. 1 st inc'd.
Cont in St st, rep Inc Row on every RS row 4 more times. 65 (66, 67, 68, 69, 69, 70, 71, 71, 72) sts.
Purl 1 WS row.
Next row (RS): Purl. (This creates a fold line for the front facing).

Peplum:
Purl 1 WS row.
Next row: Knit.
Dec Row (WS): Purl to last 4 sts, ssp, k2. 1 st dec'd.
Keeping 2 sts at edge in garter st throughout, rep Dec Row on every WS row 2 more times. 62 (63, 64, 65, 66, 66, 67, 68, 68, 69) sts.

Short Row (RS): Knit to last 5 sts, w&t.
Rep Dec Row on next row, then on foll 3 WS rows. Rep Short Row. Rep from * to * once more. 54 (55, 56, 57, 58, 58, 59, 60, 60, 61) sts.
Rep Dec Row on next row. 53 (54, 55, 56, 57, 57, 58, 59, 59, 60) sts.
Work 1 RS row even.

Pocket opening:
Next row (WS): P15, turn.
Cont on these 15 sts only, work even in St st for 31 rows, ending with a RS row. Place sts on holder.

Rejoin yarn to rem 38 (39, 40, 41, 42, 42, 43, 44, 44, 45) sts.
Row 1 (WS): Purl to last 2 sts, k2.
Row 2 (RS): K2, sl 1, knit to end.
Row 3: Purl to last 4 sts, ssp, k2. 37 (38, 39, 40, 41, 41, 42, 43, 43, 44) sts.
Row 4: Rep Row 2.
Row 5: Rep Row 1.
Row 6 (short row): K2, sl 1, knit to last 5 sts, w&t.

Row 7: Purl to last 4 sts, ssp, k2. 1 st dec'd.
Row 8: K2, sl 1, knit to end.
Row 9: Purl to last 2 sts, k2.
Row 10: Rep Row 8.
Row 11: Rep Row 7. 1 st dec'd.
Row 12: Rep Row 8.

Row 13: Rep Row 9.
Row 14 (short row): K2, sl 1, knit to last 5 sts, w&t.
Rep Rows 7–14 three more times, then Rows 7–9 once. 28 (29, 30, 31, 32, 32, 33, 34, 34, 35) sts.

Next row (RS): K2, sl 1, knit to end, place 15 sts from holder on left needle with RS facing and knit across. 43 (44, 45, 46, 47, 47, 48, 49, 49, 50) sts.

Peplum continues:
Next row (WS): Purl to last 2 sts, k2.
Short Row (RS): K2, sl 1, knit to last 5 sts, w&t.

Cont in St st, slipping the 3rd st on every RS row and keeping 2 sts at edge in garter st, rep Short Row every 8 rows 6 (7, 9, 10, 11, 12, 13, 14, 16, 17) more times.

Work even until shorter edge of peplum measures 13.75 (15.25, 16, 17.5, 18.25, 19, 20.5, 21.25, 22.5, 23.25)" / 35.5 (39, 41, 44.5, 46.5, 48, 52, 53.5, 57, 59) cm from facing fold line, ending with a RS row.

Next row (WS): Knit.
Place sts on holder. Cut yarn.

PEPLUM INSERT

With larger needles and MC, leaving a long tail, CO 8 sts. Work Rows 1 through 56 (58, 58, 60, 60, 60, 62, 66, 66, 66) of Peplum Insert Chart. 36 (36, 36, 38, 38, 38, 38, 40, 40, 40) sts.

Next row (RS): P7, knit to last 7 sts, p7.
Next row: Knit.
BO all sts pwise on RS, leaving a long yarn tail.

With the long tail and RS facing, using larger needle, pick up and knit 43 (44, 45, 46, 47, 47, 48, 49, 49, 50) sts along right edge of peplum insert. With wrong sides facing each other, join to held sts of right peplum using a 3-needle BO. With the long tail from CO and RS facing, using larger needle, pick up and knit 43 (44, 45, 46, 47, 47, 48, 49, 49, 50) sts along left edge of peplum insert. With wrong sides facing, join to held sts of left peplum using a 3-needle BO.

POCKET BAGS

Using smaller needle and CC, with RS facing, pick up and knit 31 sts from top edge of pocket opening. Beg with a WS row, work in St st for 59 rows. Leave sts on needle.

Using another smaller needle and CC, with RS facing, pick up and knit 31 sts from lower edge of pocket opening. Holding this needle together with first needle, with wrong sides of fabrics facing each other, join using a 3-needle BO.

Sew up the sides of the pocket bag using an overcasting stitch.

POCKET FLAPS

Using smaller needle and MC, with RS facing, pick up 34 sts from peplum fabric just above top edge of pocket opening, centered over opening. Work in seed st for 13 rows.

Next row (RS): Work 16 sts in patt, BO 2 sts, work to end in patt.
Next row (WS): Work in patt to bound-off sts, use the cable method to CO 2 sts, work to end.
Work 7 more rows in seed st, ending with a RS row.

Next row: Ssk, work in patt to last 2 sts, k2tog. 32 sts.
Rep the last row once more. 30 sts.
BO in patt.

JACKET BODY

With RS facing, using larger circular needle and MC, pick up 10 sts along top edge of right front peplum facing (10th st is picked up from top of purl fold line), 76 (84, 89, 97, 101, 104, 113, 116, 125, 128) sts along top edge of right peplum, 5 sts along top edge of peplum insert, 77 (85, 88, 96, 100, 105, 112, 117, 124, 129) sts along top edge of left peplum, and 10 sts along top edge of left front peplum facing (1st st is picked up from top of purl fold line). 178 (194, 202, 218, 226, 234, 250, 258, 274, 282) sts.

Row 1 (WS): Purl.
Row 2 (short row): K9, sl 1 (fold line for facing), k19 (21, 22, 24, 25, 26, 28, 29, 31, 32), pm, sl 1, pm, k19 (21, 22, 24, 25, 26, 28, 29, 31, 32), w&t.

Row 3: Purl.
Row 4 (short row): K9, sl 1, knit to m, sm, sl 1, sm, k22 (24, 25, 27, 28, 29, 31, 32, 34, 35), w&t.

Row 5: Purl.
Row 6: K9, sl 1, knit to m, sm, sl 1, sm, k39 (43, 45, 49, 51, 53, 57, 59, 63, 65), pm, sl 1, pm, k38 (42, 44, 48, 50, 52, 56, 58, 62, 64), pm, sl 1, pm, k39 (43, 45, 49, 51, 53, 57, 59, 63, 65), pm, sl 1, pm, k19 (21, 22, 24, 25, 26, 28, 29, 31, 32), sl 1 (fold line for facing), k9.

Row 7 (short row): P49 (53, 55, 59, 61, 63, 67, 69, 73, 75), w&t.
Row 8: Knit to m, sm, sl 1, sm, knit to last 10 sts, sl 1, k9.

Row 9 (short row): P52 (56, 58, 62, 64, 66, 70, 72, 76, 78), w&t.
Row 10: Rep Row 8.

Row 11: Purl to end.
Row 12: K9, sl 1, [knit to m, sm, sl 1, sm] 4 times, knit to last 10 sts, sl 1, k9.
Row 13: Purl to end.
Rep Rows 12–13 five more times.

Inc Row (RS): K9, sl 1, [knit to 1 st before m, kfb, sm, sl 1, sm, kfb] 4 times, knit to last 10 sts, sl 1, k9. 8 sts inc'd.

Continuing to slip sts as est on every RS row, rep Inc Row on every 14th row 2 more times. 202 (218, 226, 242, 250, 258, 274, 282, 298, 306) sts.
Purl 1 WS row.

Shape neck:
BO 9 sts at beg of next 2 rows. 184 (200, 208, 224, 232, 240, 256, 264, 280, 288) sts.
Discontinue the slipped sts and remove the markers.

Dec Row (RS): K1, ssk, knit to last 3 sts, k2tog, k1. 2 sts dec'd.
Rep Dec Row on every 4th row 3 more times. 176 (192, 200, 216, 224, 232, 248, 256, 272, 380) sts.

Work 2 rows even, ending with a RS row.

LEFT FRONT

Next row (WS): P42 (46, 48, 52, 54, 56, 60, 62, 66, 68), turn. Place rem unworked sts on hold for back and right front.

Next row (RS): BO 4 sts, knit to last 3 sts, k2tog, k1.

Cont to dec 1 st at neck edge on every 4th row 11 (12, 12, 13, 13, 14, 14, 15, 16, 16) more times, and **at the same time**, shape armhole:

BO 3 sts at beg of next RS row, then BO 2 sts at beg of foll 1 (2, 2, 4, 5, 5, 6, 6, 7, 7) RS rows.
Purl 1 WS row.

Armhole Dec Row (RS): K1, ssk, work to end. 1 st dec'd at armhole.
Rep Armhole Dec Row on every RS row 0 (1, 2, 1, 0, 1, 2, 3, 2, 2) more times.

Work 25 (25, 23, 25, 25, 27, 23, 25, 29, 29) rows without shaping at armhole edge, ending with a WS row.

Inc Row (RS): K1, kfb, work to end. 1 st inc'd at armhole.
Continuing to work neck decs as est, rep Inc Row on every RS row 7 more times. When all neck and armhole shaping is complete, 28 (28, 29, 29, 30, 30, 31, 31, 33, 35) sts rem.

Shape shoulder:

Row 1 (WS): Purl to last 5 (5, 6, 6, 6, 6, 6, 6, 6, 7) sts, w&t.
Row 2 (RS): Knit to last 3 sts, k2tog, k1. 1 st dec'd.

Row 3: Purl to 5 (5, 5, 5, 6, 6, 6, 6, 6, 7) sts before previous wrapped st, w&t.
Row 4: Rep Row 2.

Row 5: Purl to 5 (5, 5, 5, 5, 5, 6, 6, 6, 6) sts before previous wrapped st, w&t.
Row 6: Rep Row 2.

Row 7: Purl to 5 (5, 5, 5, 5, 5, 5, 5, 6, 6) sts before previous wrapped st, w&t.
Row 8: Knit.
Row 9: Purl to end.
Place rem 25 (25, 26, 26, 27, 27, 28, 28, 30, 32) sts on a holder.

RIGHT FRONT

Transfer 42 (46, 48, 52, 54, 56, 60, 62, 66, 68) sts from end of holder to needle and join yarn with RS facing. Knit 1 RS row.

Next row (WS): BO 4 sts, purl to last 3 sts, ssp, p1.

Cont to dec 1 st at neck edge on every 4th row 11 (12, 12, 13, 13, 14, 14, 15, 16, 16) more times, and **at the same time**, shape armhole:
BO 3 sts at beg of next WS row, then BO 2 sts at beg of foll 1 (2, 2, 4, 5, 5, 6, 6, 7, 7) WS rows.
Work 1 RS row even.

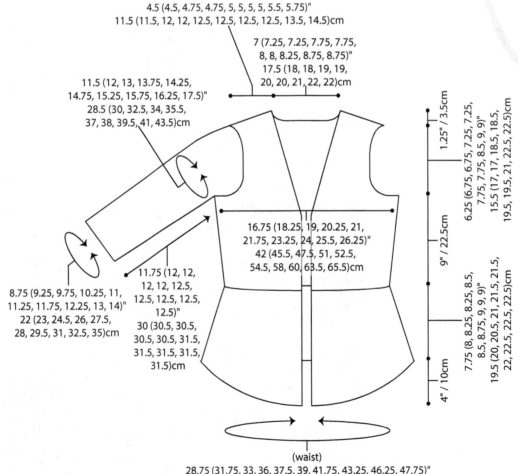

4.5 (4.5, 4.75, 4.75, 5, 5, 5, 5, 5.5, 5.75)"
11.5 (11.5, 12, 12, 12.5, 12.5, 12.5, 12.5, 13.5, 14.5)cm

7 (7.25, 7.25, 7.75, 7.75, 8, 8, 8.25, 8.75, 8.75)"
17.5 (18, 18, 19, 19, 20, 20, 21, 22, 22)cm

11.5 (12, 13, 13.75, 14.25, 14.75, 15.25, 15.75, 16.25, 17.5)"
28.5 (30, 32.5, 34, 35.5, 37, 38, 39.5, 41, 43.5)cm

1.25" / 3.5cm

6.25 (6.75, 6.75, 7.25, 7.25, 7.75, 7.75, 8.5, 9, 9)"
15.5 (17, 17, 18.5, 18.5, 19.5, 19.5, 21, 22.5, 22.5)cm

16.75 (18.25, 19, 20.25, 21, 21.75, 23.25, 24, 25.5, 26.25)"
42 (45.5, 47.5, 51, 52.5, 54.5, 58, 60, 63.5, 65.5)cm

9" / 22.5cm

8.75 (9.25, 9.75, 10.25, 11, 11.25, 11.75, 12.25, 13, 14)"
22 (23, 24.5, 26, 27.5, 28, 29.5, 31, 32.5, 35)cm

11.75 (12, 12, 12, 12, 12.5, 12.5, 12.5, 12.5, 12.5)"
30 (30.5, 30.5, 30.5, 30.5, 31.5, 31.5, 31.5, 31.5, 31.5)cm

7.75 (8, 8.25, 8.25, 8.5, 8.5, 8.75, 9, 9, 9)"
19.5 (20, 20.5, 21, 21.5, 21.5, 22, 22.5, 22.5, 22.5)cm

4" / 10cm

(waist)
28.75 (31.75, 33, 36, 37.5, 39, 41.75, 43.25, 46.25, 47.75)"
72 (79, 82.5, 90, 93.5, 97.5, 104.5, 108, 115.5, 119)cm

Armhole Dec Row (WS): P1, p2tog, work to end. 1 st dec'd at armhole.
Rep Armhole Dec Row on every WS row 0 (1, 2, 1, 0, 1, 2, 3, 2, 2) more times.

Work 25 (25, 23, 25, 25, 27, 23, 25, 29, 29) rows without shaping at armhole edge, ending with a RS row.

Inc Row (WS): P1, pfb, work to end. 1 st inc'd at armhole.
Continuing to work neck decs as est, rep Inc Row on every WS row 7 more times. When all neck and armhole shaping is complete, 28 (28, 29, 29, 30, 30, 31, 31, 33, 35) sts rem.

Shape shoulder:
Row 1 (RS): Knit to last 5 (5, 6, 6, 6, 6, 6, 6, 6, 7) sts, w&t.
Row 2 (WS): Purl to last 3 sts, ssp, p1. 1 st dec'd.

Row 3: Knit to 5 (5, 5, 5, 6, 6, 6, 6, 6, 7) sts before previous wrapped st, w&t.
Row 4: Rep Row 2.

Row 5: K1, ssk, knit to 5 (5, 5, 5, 5, 6, 6, 6, 6) sts before previous wrapped st, w&t.
Row 6: Rep Row 2. 1 st dec'd.

Row 7: Knit to 5 (5, 5, 5, 5, 5, 5, 6, 6) sts before previous wrapped st, w&t.
Row 8: Purl.
Row 9: Knit to end.
Place rem 25 (25, 26, 26, 27, 27, 28, 28, 30, 32) sts on a holder.

BACK

Transfer rem 92 (100, 104, 112, 116, 120, 128, 132, 140, 144) sts from holder to needle and join yarn with RS facing.

BO 4 sts at beg of next 2 rows, then BO 3 sts at beg of foll 2 rows, then BO 2 sts at beg of foll 2 (4, 4, 8, 10, 10, 12, 12, 14, 14) rows. 74 (78, 82, 82, 82, 86, 90, 94, 98, 102) sts.

Dec Row (RS): K1, ssk, knit to last 3 sts, k2tog, k1. 2 sts dec'd.
Rep Dec Row on every RS row 0 (1, 2, 1, 0, 1, 2, 3, 2, 2) more times. 72 (74, 76, 78, 80, 82, 84, 86, 92, 96) sts.

Work 25 (25, 23, 25, 25, 27, 23, 25, 29, 29) rows even, ending with a WS row.

Inc Row (RS): K1, kfb, knit to last 2 sts, kfb, k1. 2 sts inc'd.

Rep Inc Row on every RS row 7 more times. 88 (90, 92, 94, 96, 98, 100, 102, 108, 112) sts.

Shape neck and shoulders:
Row 1 (WS): Purl to last 5 (5, 6, 6, 6, 6, 6, 6, 6, 7) sts, w&t.
Row 2 (RS): Knit to last 5 (5, 6, 6, 6, 6, 6, 6, 6, 7) sts, w&t.

Left side:
Row 3: P26 (26, 26, 26, 27, 27, 28, 28, 30, 31), turn.
Row 4 (RS): BO 3 sts, knit to 5 (5, 5, 5, 6, 6, 6, 6, 6, 7) sts before previous wrapped st, w&t. 28 (28, 29, 29, 30, 30, 31, 31, 33, 35) sts.

Row 5: Purl.
Row 6: BO 2 sts, knit to 5 (5, 5, 5, 5, 5, 6, 6, 6, 6) sts before previous wrapped st, w&t. 26 (26, 27, 27, 28, 28, 29, 29, 31, 33) sts.

Row 7: Purl.
Row 8: K1, ssk, knit to 5 (5, 5, 5, 5, 5, 5, 5, 6, 6) sts before previous wrapped st, w&t. 25 (25, 26, 26, 27, 27, 28, 28, 30, 32) sts.
Row 9: Purl.
Row 10: Knit to end.
Place sts on holder.

Right side:
With WS facing, place next 26 (28, 28, 30, 30, 32, 32, 34, 36, 36) sts on holder. Join yarn to rem 31 (31, 32, 32, 33, 33, 34, 34, 36, 38) sts with WS facing.

Row 3 (WS): BO 3 sts, purl to 5 (5, 5, 5, 6, 6, 6, 6, 6, 7) sts before previous wrapped st, w&t. 28 (28, 29, 29, 30, 30, 31, 31, 33, 35) sts.
Row 4: Knit.

Row 5: BO 2 sts, purl to 5 (5, 5, 5, 5, 5, 6, 6, 6, 6) sts before previous wrapped st, w&t. 26 (26, 27, 27, 28, 28, 29, 29, 31, 33) sts.
Row 6: Knit.

Row 7: P1, p2tog, purl to 5 (5, 5, 5, 5, 5, 5, 5, 6, 6) sts before previous wrapped st, w&t. 25 (25, 26, 26, 27, 27, 28, 28, 30, 32) sts.
Row 8: Knit.
Row 9: Purl to end.
Place sts on holder.

Join front and back shoulders using a 3-needle BO.

COLLAR

With smaller circular needle and using MC, with RS facing, beg in slipped-st facing fold line, pick up and knit 71 (75, 75, 79, 79, 83, 83, 89, 89, 93) sts along right front neckline, 5 sts along back neck slope, purl across 26 (28, 28, 30, 30, 32, 32, 34, 36, 36) sts from back neck st holder, pick up and knit 5 sts along back neck slope, and 71 (75, 75, 79, 79, 83, 83, 89, 89, 93) sts along left front neckline, ending in slipped-st facing fold line. 178 (188, 188, 198, 198, 208, 208, 222, 224, 232) sts.

Working in seed st, work 2 rows even.

Shape collar with short rows:
Rows 1–2: Work in patt to last 6 sts, w&t.
Rows 3–4: Work in patt to 6 sts before previous wrapped st, w&t.
Rows 5–7: Work in patt to 4 sts before previous wrapped st, w&t.

Change to larger needle.
Rows 8–24: Work in patt to 4 sts before previous wrapped st, w&t.
Row 25: Work in patt to end.
BO all sts in patt.

RIGHT SLEEVE

With RS facing, using shorter US #6 / 4mm circular needle and MC, beg at center underarm, pick up and knit 63 (66, 72, 75, 78, 81, 84, 87, 90, 96) sts evenly around armhole. Pm and join to work in the round.

Shape cap with short rows:
Row 1 (RS): K42 (44, 48, 50, 52, 54, 56, 58, 60, 64), w&t.
Row 2: P21 (22, 24, 25, 26, 27, 28, 29, 30, 32), w&t.

Row 3: Knit to and including previous wrapped st, w&t.
Row 4: Purl to and including previous wrapped st, w&t.
Rep Rows 3–4 15 (16, 18, 19, 20, 21, 22, 23, 24, 26) more times.

Next rnd: Knit to end of rnd.
Continuing in the rnd, work 2 rnds even.

Dec Rnd: K2tog, knit to end. 1 st dec'd.

Changing to dpns when necessary, rep Dec Rnd on every 6 (6, 5, 5, 5, 5, 5, 5, 5, 5)th rnd 14 (14, 17, 17, 17, 18, 18, 18, 18, 18) more times. 48 (51, 54, 57, 60, 62, 65, 68, 71, 77) sts.

Work even, if necessary, until sleeve measures 11.75 (12, 12, 12, 12, 12.5, 12.5, 12.5, 12.5, 12.5)" / 30 (30.5, 30.5, 30.5, 30.5, 31.5, 31.5, 31.5, 31.5) cm from underarm. Leave sts on needle.

Cuff:
With larger needle, CO 48 (51, 54, 57, 60, 62, 65, 68, 71, 77) sts. Work in seed st for 30 rows.

With the right sides facing, join cuff to sleeve sts using a 3-needle BO.

LEFT SLEEVE

Work as for Right Sleeve, except work Dec Rnd as: Knit to last 2 sts, k2tog.

BUTTON TABS (MAKE 3)

With smaller needles and MC, CO 12 sts. Work Row 1 of Tabs and Epaulettes Chart once, then work Rows 2–21 twice, then work Rows 22–40 once. BO in patt.

EPAULETTES (MAKE 2) AND BACK PLEAT TAB (MAKE 1)

With smaller needles and MC, CO 12 sts. Work Row 1 of Tabs and Epaulettes Chart once, then work Rows 2–21 twice, then Rows 22–32 once, then Rows 33–34 four times. BO in patt.

FINISHING

Fold front facings to inside and slip stitch in place, taking care that sts do not show on RS.

Sew ends of collar to inside of jacket. Weave in ends.

Sew a button to each end of cuffs, through the cuff and the sleeve, to hold the cuff in position.

Sew a button to each pocket to correspond with buttonholes, through the jacket and the top layer of the pocket bag, which will help the pocket lie flat.

Sew ends of epaulettes to the shoulder at the sleeve join, centered over the shoulder seam. Sew a button to the opposite end of the epaulette, through the epaulette and the jacket.

Block jacket before attaching tabs, to ensure even placement. When blocking, ensure the pocket bags are flat, the collar is sitting correctly, the peplum insert is lying flat and even and the bottom edge of the peplum is flat.

Position first button tab at the top of the jacket, just below the base of the neckline. Second button tab goes just above the waistline seam. Third button tab should be centered between the first two. Slip stitch around all edges of the half of the tab without the buttonhole, securing it to one side of the garment. Leave the end with the buttonhole free. Sew buttons to jacket to correspond with buttonholes, then sew matching buttons to stitched-down ends of the tabs, through the tab and the jacket.

Position the back pleat tab on the jacket just above the waist seam, centered over the peplum insert. Sew a button to each end, through the tab and the jacket.

TABS AND EPAULETTES CHART

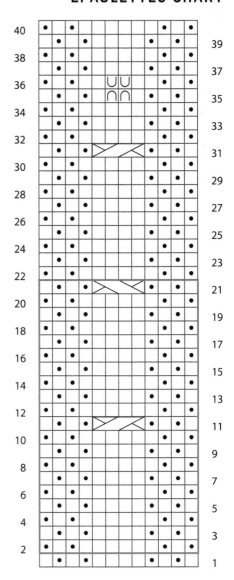

	RS: knit; WS: purl		Y	kfb
•	RS: purl; WS: knit		Ƴ	pfb
∩	bind off		M	make 1 purl/M1P
U	cast on			
	pattern repeat			

✕ 2/2 LC: sl 2 to cn, hold to front, k2, k2 from cn

✕ 2/2 RC: sl 2 to cn, hold to back, k2, k2 from cn

PEPLUM INSERT CHART

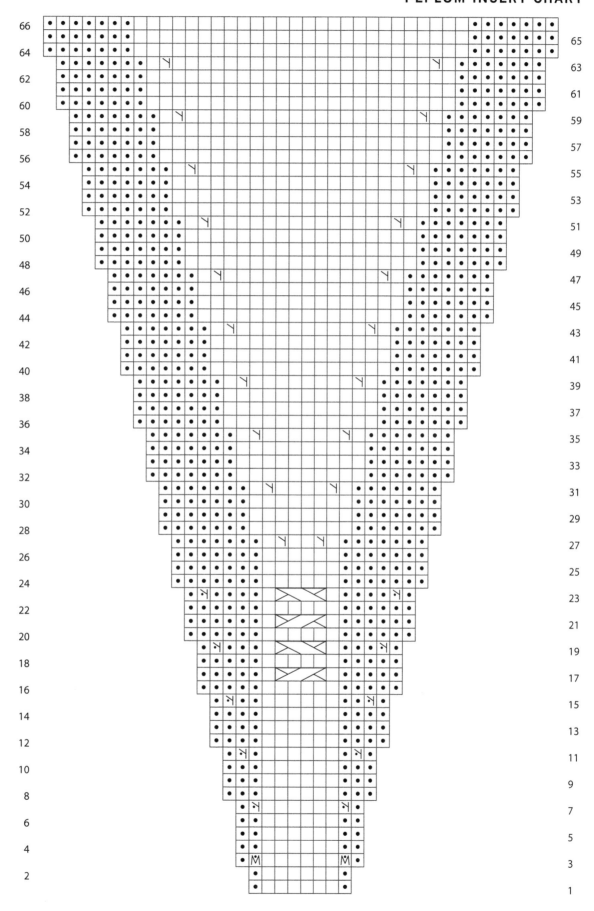

Utility Corset

Rachel Anderson

It is a truth universally acknowledged, that a young lady dispossessed by calamity of her maid, must be in want of a Utility Corset....

The Utility Corset is inspired by handymen's utility belts—deceptively simple in construction, easy to put on, and with lots of hidden pockets and storage loops. Ideal for the post-apocalyptic heroine who needs to keep her equipment to hand and her hands free!

PATTERN NOTES

The corset is knit flat from the bottom up, using a crochet chain cast on to create an edge that matches the bind-off edge. It is constructed in one piece but has the appearance of individually-worked panels, which provide the shaping. The panels, in order of working on Row 1, are:

- Placket (PL)—this is tucked underneath when worn, and hides a secret pocket.
- Back Panel 1 (B1)
- Side Panel 1 (S1)
- Front Panel 1 (F1)
- Front Panel 2 (F2)
- Side Panel 2 (S2)
- Back Panel 2 (B2)

Seed stitch is worked on the first and last 5 sts on each row, and on the first and last 7 rows of the garment.

The corset is laced with three purled i-cords which are tied around the body. Further i-cord loops are sewn onto the points on the lower hem.

The corset pattern as written has three hidden pockets. These are based on Elizabeth Zimmermann's Afterthought pocket, but here the pockets are put in place during knitting, rather than afterward. However, several potential pockets can be prepared, and any that are not required can be easily hidden again. Good positions for pockets are on the hip or bodice portions of the side panels, the bodice portions of other panels, and, of course, the placket.

STITCHES AND TECHNIQUES

SEED STITCH

(Worked flat, mult of 2 sts)
Row 1 (RS): [K1, p1] to end.

Row 2 (WS): [P1, k1] to end.
Rep Rows 1–2.

(Worked flat, mult of 2 sts + 1)
Row 1: [K1, p1] to last st, k1.
Rep Row 1.

EYELET

(Worked over 3 sts and 2 rows)
Row 1 (RS): Sl 1 kwise, k1 but do not remove st from left needle, pass sl st over knit st, yo, pass 2nd st on left needle over first st, k1.
Row 2 (WS): P1, purl into st below yo, p1.

IMPROVED SSK (ISSK)

Sl 1 kwise, sl 1 pwise, insert left needle through front of sts and k2tog tbl.

SIZES

Women's XXS (XS, S, M, L, XL, 2X, 3X, 4X, 5X); shown in size XS.

Intended to be worn with 3" / 7.5 cm of negative ease

FINISHED MEASUREMENTS

All measurements are with the corset closed, back panel fully overlapping placket.

Hip: 31.25 (33.5, 35.25, 37.5, 39.75, 41, 44.25, 48.25, 52.25, 56.75)" / 78.5 (84, 88.5, 94, 99.5, 103, 110.5, 120.5, 130.5, 141.5)cm

Waist: 21.5 (23.75, 25.5, 27.75, 30, 31.25, 34.5, 38.5, 42.5, 47)" / 54 (59.5, 64, 69.5, 75, 78.5, 86, 96, 106, 117)cm

Underbust: 21.5 (23.75, 25.5, 27.75, 32.25, 35.75, 37.5, 39.25, 43.25, 47.75)" / 54 (59.5, 64, 69.5, 80.5, 89.5, 94, 98.5, 108.5, 119.5)cm

MATERIALS

Donegal Yarns Aran Tweed (100% wool; 87yds / 80m per 50g skein); color: 4826 Espresso; 7 (7, 8, 8, 9, 9, 10, 10, 11, 12) skeins

32-inch US #6 / 4mm circular needle, or size needed to obtain gauge
Set of US #6 / 4mm dpns
US G / 4mm crochet hook

Stitch markers, yarn needle

GAUGE

18 sts and 28 rows = 4" / 10cm in St st

AFTERTHOUGHT POCKET SET-UP

Work to the desired pocket location. Using a separate length of yarn, knit the required number of sts for the pocket. Drop the separate length of yarn and switch to main yarn. Stranding main yarn very loosely behind the pocket sts on the WS, work the remainder of the row.

Note: This is usually performed with a piece of contrasting waste yarn, but by using a separate piece of the main yarn you have the option of putting in the pocket later, or changing your mind and leaving the fabric intact with no one the wiser.

PATTERN

Using the crochet chain method and circular needle, CO 171 (181, 193, 204, 216, 222, 240, 263, 281, 308) sts. Work in seed st for 7 rows.

Set-up row (WS): Work 5 sts in seed st, p25 (25, 29, 30, 32, 32, 36, 41, 41, 48) [PL], pm, k1, pm, p24 (26, 28, 29, 31, 32, 35, 40, 44, 48) [B1], pm, p3, pm, p10 (10, 10, 14, 14, 16, 16, 16, 16, 16) [S1], pm, p3, pm, p26 (29, 31, 31, 34, 34, 38, 42, 47, 53) [F1], pm, p3, pm, p26 (29, 31, 31, 34, 34, 38, 42, 47, 53) [F2], pm, p3, pm, p10 (10, 10, 14, 14, 16, 16, 16, 16, 16) [S2], pm, p3, pm, p24 (26, 28, 29, 31, 32, 35, 40, 44, 48), work 5 sts in seed st [B2].

HIP

Row 1 (RS): Work 5 sts in seed st, [knit to m, sm, work Row 1 of eyelet, sm] 5 times, knit to next m, sm, p1, sm, knit to last 5 sts, work seed st to end.

Row 2 (WS): Work 5 sts in seed st, purl to first m, sm, k1, sm, [purl to m, sm, work Row 2 of eyelet, sm] 5 times, purl to last 5 sts, work seed st to end.

Rep Rows 1–2 4 (4, 4, 4, 8, 8, 8, 8, 8, 8) more times. Note: seed st edges, single purl st "seam" between PL and B1, and eyelet "seamlines" between other panels continue throughout garment.

Next row (RS): Work in est patt to 4th m, sm (you are now on panel F2), [issk, knit to 2 sts before m, k2tog, sm, work eyelet, sm] 2 times, work in est patt to end. 4 sts dec'd: 2 sts each front panel.

Work 5 rows even.
Dec Row (RS): Work 5 sts in patt, issk, knit to 2 sts before m, k2tog, sm, work eyelet, sm, knit to next m, sm, work eyelet, sm, [issk, knit to 2 sts before m, k2tog, sm, work eyelet, sm] twice, knit to m, sm, work eyelet, sm, issk, knit to 2 sts before m, k2tog, sm, p1, sm, issk, knit to last 7 sts, k2tog, work in patt to end. 10 sts dec'd: 2 sts each front panel, 2 sts each back panel, and 2 sts on placket.

Rep Dec Row on every 6th row 4 more times, working an afterthought pocket set-up on the center 8 sts of panel S1

on the last row. 117 (127, 139, 150, 162, 168, 186, 209, 227, 254) sts: 20 (20, 24, 25, 27, 27, 31, 36, 36, 43) in placket, 1 purled "seam" st, 14 (16, 18, 19, 21, 22, 25, 30, 34, 38) in B1 panel, 10 (10, 10, 14, 14, 16, 16, 16, 16, 16) each side panel, 14 (17, 19, 19, 22, 22, 26, 30, 35, 41) each front panel, 19 (21, 23, 24, 26, 27, 30, 35, 39, 43) in B2 panel, and 5 "seamlines" of 3 sts each.

BODICE

Sizes XXS (XS, S, M) only:
Continuing to work eyelet "seamlines," single purl st between PL and B1, and seed st edges throughout, work 35 rows even, ending with a WS row.
Next row: Work in est patt, working an afterthought pocket set-up on center 8 sts of panels F2 and PL on the last row. Work 1 row even.
Work in seed st over all sts for 7 rows. BO.

Size L only:
Continuing to work eyelet "seamlines," single purl st between PL and B1, and seed st edges throughout, work 29 rows even, ending with a WS row.
Next row (RS): Work 5 sts in patt, m1, knit to m, m1, sm, work eyelet, sm, knit to m, sm, work eyelet, sm, [m1, knit to m, m1, sm, work eyelet, sm] twice, knit to m, sm, work eyelet, sm, m1, knit to m, m1, sm, p1, sm, m1, knit to last 5 sts, m1, work in patt to end. 172 sts: 29 placket sts, 1 purl "seam" st, 23 in

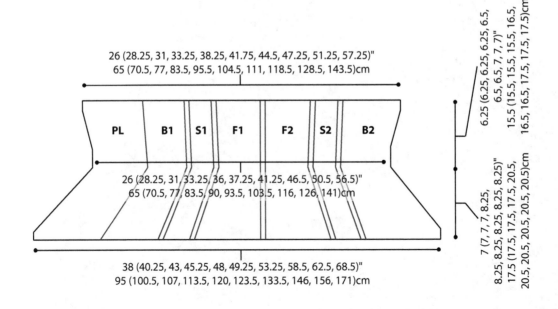

26 (28.25, 31, 33.25, 38.25, 41.75, 44.5, 47.25, 51.25, 57.25)"
65 (70.5, 77, 83.5, 95.5, 104.5, 111, 118.5, 128.5, 143.5)cm

| PL | B1 | S1 | F1 | F2 | S2 | B2 |

6.25 (6.25, 6.25, 6.25, 6.5, 6.5, 6.5, 7, 7, 7)"
15.5 (15.5, 15.5, 15.5, 16.5, 16.5, 16.5, 17.5, 17.5, 17.5)cm

26 (28.25, 31, 33.25, 36, 37.25, 41.25, 46.5, 50.5, 56.5)"
65 (70.5, 77, 83.5, 90, 93.5, 103.5, 116, 126, 141)cm

7 (7, 7, 7, 8.25, 8.25, 8.25, 8.25, 8.25, 8.25)"
17.5 (17.5, 17.5, 17.5, 20.5, 20.5, 20.5, 20.5, 20.5, 20.5)cm

38 (40.25, 43, 45.25, 48, 49.25, 53.25, 58.5, 62.5, 68.5)"
95 (100.5, 107, 113.5, 120, 123.5, 133.5, 146, 156, 171)cm

B1 panel, 14 in each side panel, 24 in each front panel, 28 in B2 panel, and 5 "seamlines" of 3 sts each.

Work 7 rows even, ending with a WS row.
Next row (RS): Work in est patt, working an afterthought pocket set-up on center 8 sts of panels F2 and PL on the last row.
Work 1 row even.
Work in seed st over all sts for 7 rows.
BO.

Size XL only:
Continuing to work eyelet "seamlines," single purl st between PL and B1, and seed st edges throughout, work 19 rows even, ending with a WS row.
Inc Row (RS): Work 5 sts in patt, m1, knit to m, m1, sm, work eyelet, sm, knit to m, sm, work eyelet, sm, [m1, knit to m, m1, sm, work eyelet, sm] twice, knit to m, sm, work eyelet, sm, m1, knit to m, m1, sm, p1, sm, m1, knit to last 5 sts, m1, work in patt to end. 10 sts inc'd: 2 each front panel, 2 each back panel, and 2 on placket.

Work 9 rows even, ending with a WS row.
Rep Inc Row. 188 sts: 31 placket sts, 1 purl "seam" st, 26 in B1 panel, 16 in each side panel, 26 in each front panel, 31 in B2 panel, and 5 "seamlines" of 3 sts each.

Work 7 rows even, ending with a WS row.
Next row: Work in est patt, working an afterthought pocket set-up on center 8 sts of panels F2 and PL on the last row.

Work 1 row even.
Work in seed st over all sts for 7 rows.
BO.

Size 2X only:
Continuing to work eyelet "seamlines," single purl st between PL and B1, and seed st edges throughout, work 19 rows even, ending with a WS row.
Next row (RS): Work in patt to 4th m (you are now on panel F2), sm, [m1, knit to m, m1, sm, work eyelet, sm] twice, work in patt to end. 4 sts inc'd: 2 each front panel.

Work 9 rows even, ending with a WS row.
Next row (RS): Work 5 sts in patt, m1, knit to m, m1, sm, work eyelet, sm, knit to m, sm, work eyelet, sm, [m1, knit to m, m1, sm, work eyelet, sm] twice, knit

to m, sm, work eyelet, sm, m1, knit to m, m1, sm, p1, sm, m1, knit to last 5 sts, m1, work in patt to end. 200 sts: 33 in placket, 1 purl "seam" st, 27 in B1 panel, 16 each side panel, 30 each front panel, 32 in B2 panel, and 5 "seamlines" of 3 sts each.

Work 7 rows even, ending with a WS row.
Next row: Work in est patt, working an afterthought pocket set-up on center 8 sts of panels F2 and PL on the last row.

Work 1 row even.
Work in seed st over all sts for 7 rows.
BO.

Sizes – (–, –, –, –, –, –, 3X, 4X, 5X) only:
Continuing to work eyelet "seamlines," single purl st between PL and B1, and seed st edges throughout, work 29 rows even, ending with a WS row.
Next row (RS): Work in patt to 4th m (you are now on panel F2), sm, [m1, knit to m, m1, sm, work eyelet, sm] twice, work in patt to end. – (–, –, –, –, –, –, 213, 231, 258) sts: – (–, –, –, –, –, –, 36, 36, 43) in placket, 1 purl "seam" st, – (–, –, –, –, –, –, 30, 34, 38) in B1 panel, – (–, –, –, –, –, –, 16, 16, 16) each side panel, – (–, –, –, –, –, –, 32, 37, 43) each front panel, – (–, –, –, –, –, –, 35, 39, 43) in B2 panel, and 5 "seamlines" of 3 sts each.

Work 11 rows even, ending with a WS row.
Next row: Work in est patt, working an afterthought pocket set-up on center 8 sts of panels F2 and PL on the last row.
Work 1 row even.
Work in seed st over all sts for 7 rows.
BO.

LOOPS (MAKE 6)

With dpn, CO 4 sts. Work i-cord in purl stitch for 4" / 10cm. Fasten off.

TIES

With dpn, CO 4 sts. Work three i-cords in purl stitch, in the foll lengths:

⚮ I-cord 1 (underbust): 24 (26.5, 29, 31, 36, 40, 43, 45.5, 50.5, 55.5)" / 61 (67.5, 73.5, 78.5, 91.5, 101.5, 109, 115.5, 128.5, 141)cm.

⚮ I-cord 2 (waist): 24 (26.5, 29, 31, 34, 35.5, 39.5, 45, 49.5, 55)" / 61 (67.5, 73.5, 78.5, 86.5, 90, 100.5, 114.5, 125.5, 139.5)cm.

⚮ I-cord 3 (hip): 36 (38.5, 41, 43, 46, 47.5, 51.5, 56.5, 61.5, 66.5)" / 91.5 (98, 104, 109, 117, 120.5, 131, 143.5, 156, 169)cm.

POCKETS

Remove the extra length of yarn from the pocket sts, leaving two sets of live sts, upper and lower. The lower set of sts will be the pocket edging, and the upper sts the inner lining of the pocket. Place each set of sts onto a dpn.

Using a third dpn, join yarn and work in St st on the upper sts only until the pocket lining is the desired length. BO.

On the lower sts, join yarn and work 1 row in seed stitch. BO.

FINISHING

Loosely slip stitch the pocket lining(s) to the WS of the corset.

Stitch the three ties to the center of the seed st edging on the B2 panel, at underbust, waist, and hip levels.

Form the shorter cords into loops and sew to the WS of the seed stitch hem at the "seamlines."

Weave in ends. Block, paying particular attention to the measurements in the schematic.

Quaintrelle

Holly Priestley

What is a Quaintrelle, you ask? Why, it's a lady-dandy! And only the dandiest lady will be spotted in this divine diamond patterned vest. Just don't ask about the curious buttons—trust me, you don't want to know.

PATTERN NOTES

Vest is worked flat in one piece from the bottom up to the armholes, then divided and fronts and back are worked separately to the shoulder.

STITCHES AND TECHNIQUES

1X1 TWISTED RIB

(Multiple of 2 sts)
Row 1 (RS): [K1 tbl, p1] to end.
Row 2 (WS): [K1, p1 tbl] to end.
Rep Rows 1–2.

TEXTURE PANEL

(Worked over 27 sts)
Row 1 (RS): [K1 tbl, p1] 2 times, k1, [sl 5 pwise wyif, k1] 3 times, [p1, k1 tbl] 2 times.
Row 2 (WS): [P1 tbl, k1] 2 times, p19, [k1, p1 tbl] 2 times.
Row 3: [K1 tbl, p1] 2 times, k19, [p1, k1 tbl] 2 times.
Row 4: [P1 tbl, k1] 2 times, p1, [p2, with the right needle pick up the loose strand from Row 1, transfer it to the left needle so that it sits *after* (to the left of) the first st on left needle, p1, drop the strand from Row 1, p3] 3 times, [k1, p1 tbl] 2 times.

Row 5: [K1 tbl, p1] 2 times, k4, [sl 5 pwise wyif, k1] 2 times, k3, [p1, k1 tbl] 2 times.
Row 6: [P1 tbl, k1] 2 times, p19, [k1, p1 tbl] 2 times.
Row 7: [K1 tbl, p1] 2 times, k19, [p1, k1 tbl] 2 times.

Row 8: [P1 tbl, k1] 2 times, p6, [with the right needle pick up the loose strand from Row 5, transfer it to the left needle so that it sits *after* (to the left of) the first st on left needle, p1, drop the strand from Row 5, p5] 2 times, p1, [k1, p1 tbl] 2 times.

Rep Rows 1–8.

PATTERN

LOWER BODY

With circular needle, CO 163 (183, 203, 223) sts.
Row 1 (RS): K1, pm, [k1, p1] 2 times, k19, [p1, k1] 2 times, pm, [p1, k1] 20 (25, 30, 35) times, pm, [k1, p1] 2 times, k19, [p1, k1] 2 times, pm, [k1, p1] 20 (25, 30, 35) times, pm, [k1, p1] 2 times, k19, [p1, k1] 2 times, pm, k1.

Row 2 (WS): Sl 1, [sm, work Row 2 of Texture Panel to m, sm, work Row 2 of 1x1 Twisted Rib to m, sm] 2 times, work Row 2 of Texture Panel to m, sm, p1.

Row 3: Sl 1, [sm, work next row of Texture Panel to m, sm, work next row of 1x1 Twisted Rib to m, sm] 2 times, work next row of Texture Panel to m, sm, k1.

Continue in est patt, slipping the first st of every row, until work measures 1.5" / 4cm, ending with a WS row.

Next row (RS): Sl 1, [sm, work next row of Texture Panel to m, sm, work in Reverse St st to m, sm] 2 times, work next row of Texture panel to m, sm, k1.

Continue in est patt until work measures about 2" / 5cm, ending with Row 1 of Texture Panel.

Shape waist:
Dec Row (WS): Work in patt to second m, sm, k9 (11, 13, 15), k2tog, work in patt to 11 (13, 15, 17) sts before fifth m, ssk, work in patt to end. 2 sts dec'd.

Rep Dec Row on every 6th row 3 more times. 155 (175, 195, 215) sts. Work 1 row even, ending with Row 3 of Texture Panel.

SIZES

Women's S (M, L, XL); shown in size S

Intended to be worn with 1–2" / 2.5–5cm of positive ease

FINISHED MEASUREMENTS

Bust: 30.25 (34.25, 38.25, 42.25)" / 75.5 (85.5, 95.5, 105.5)cm

MATERIALS

Malabrigo Merino Worsted (100% merino wool; 210 yds / 192m per 100g skein); color: Pale Khaki; 4 (5, 5, 6) skeins

32-inch US #10 / 6mm circular needle, or size needed to obtain gauge US #10 / 6mm dpns

Stitch markers, stitch holders, yarn needle, scrap yarn, three 2" / 5cm toggle buttons

GAUGE

20 sts and 28 rows = 4" / 10cm in Reverse St st

Pocket openings (WS):
Work 9 sts in patt. With scrap yarn, work next 11 sts in patt, turn (RS is facing). P11, turn (WS is facing). Change back to working yarn, k11, work in patt to last 20 sts. With scrap yarn, work next 11 sts in patt, turn (RS is facing). P11, turn (WS is facing). Change back to working yarn, k11, work in patt to end.

Work 3 rows even. Rep Dec Row on next row, then every foll 6th row 3 more times. 147 (167, 187, 207) sts.

Work even until work measures 10" / 25.5cm, ending with a RS row.

Inc Row (WS): Work in patt to second m, sm, k9 (11, 13, 15), kfb, work in patt to 10 (12, 14, 16) sts before fifth m, kfb, work in patt to end. 2 sts inc'd.

Work 11 rows even, then rep Inc Row. 151 (171, 191, 211) sts.

Work even until work measures 14.5 (15, 15, 15.5)" / 37 (38, 38, 39.5)cm, ending with a WS row.

Divide for fronts and back (RS):
Work 36 (38, 40, 42) sts in patt and place on a holder for left front, work 79 (95, 111, 127) sts in patt, place rem 36 (38, 40, 42) sts on a holder for right front. 79 (95, 111, 127) sts rem on needle for back.

BACK

Shape armholes:
Row 1 (WS): Sl 1, ssk, work in patt to last 3 sts, k2tog, k1. 2 sts dec'd.
Row 2 (RS): Sl 1, work in patt to end.
Rep the last 2 rows 9 (7, 5, 1) more time(s), then WS row once more. 57 (77, 97, 121) sts.

Next row (RS): Sl 1, p2tog, work in patt to last 3 sts, p2tog tbl, p1. 2 sts dec'd.
Next row (WS): Sl 1, ssk, work in patt to last 3 sts, k2tog, k1. 2 sts dec'd.
Rep the last 2 rows 4 (9, 14, 20) more times. 37 sts.

Shape neck:
Row 1 (RS): Sl 1, p2tog, work 15 sts in patt, kfb, sl 1 st from right needle to left, place rem 19 sts on left needle on a holder for left side, turn work. 18 sts rem for right side.

Row 2: Sl 1, ssk, work in patt to last 3 sts, k2tog, k1. 16 sts.

Work 5 rows even, then place these 16 sts on holder for shoulder.

Return 19 held left side sts to needle and join yarn with RS facing.

Row 1 (RS): Work to last 3 sts, p2tog tbl, p1. 18 sts.
Row 2: Sl 1, ssk, work in patt to last 3 sts, k2tog, k1. 16 sts.

Work 6 rows even, then place these 16 sts on holder for shoulder.

RIGHT FRONT

Return 36 (38, 40, 42) right front sts to needle and join yarn with WS facing.

Shape armhole:
Slipping the first st of every row, work 4 rows even.
Dec Row (WS): Sl 1, ssk, work in patt to end. 1 st dec'd.
Rep Dec Row on every 4th row 5 (7, 9, 11) more times. 30 sts.
Work even, continuing to slip the first st of every row, until armhole measures 7 (7.5, 7.75, 8)" / 18 (19, 19.5, 20.5)cm, ending with a WS row.

Shape neck:
Row 1 (RS): Work 6 sts in patt, ssk, work in patt to 7 sts before m, k2tog, work to end. 28 sts.

Rows 2, 4, 6, 8 (WS): Work even.
Row 3: Rep Row 1. 26 sts.

Row 5: Sl 1, sm, k3tog, p1, k1, ssk, work in patt to 7 sts before m, k2tog, work to end. 22 sts.

Row 7: Sl 1, sm, k1 tbl, p1, k1, ssk, work in patt to 7 sts before m, k2tog, work to end. 20 sts.

Row 9: K3tog, k1, ssk, k5, k2tog, work in patt to end. 16 sts.
Graft the right front and right back shoulder sts together.

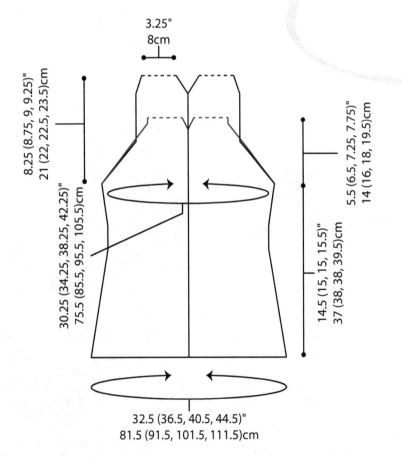

3.25"
8cm

8.25 (8.75, 9, 9.25)"
21 (22, 22.5, 23.5)cm

30.25 (34.25, 38.25, 42.25)"
75.5 (85.5, 95.5, 105.5)cm

5.5 (6.5, 7.25, 7.75)"
14 (16, 18, 19.5)cm

14.5 (15, 15, 15.5)"
37 (38, 38, 39.5)cm

32.5 (36.5, 40.5, 44.5)"
81.5 (91.5, 101.5, 111.5)cm

LEFT FRONT

Return 36 (38, 40, 42) left front sts to needle and join yarn with WS facing.

Shape armhole:
Slipping the first st of every row, work 4 rows even.
Dec Row (WS): Work in patt to last 3 sts, k2tog, k1. 1 st dec'd.
Rep Dec Row on every 4th row 5 (7, 9, 11) more times. 30 sts.
Work even, continuing to slip the first st of every row, until armhole measures 7 (7.5, 7.75, 8)" / 18 (19, 19.5, 20.5)cm, ending with a WS row.

Shape neck:
Row 1 (RS): Work to m, sm, work 5 sts in patt, ssk, work in patt to 7 sts before m, k2tog, work to end. 28 sts.

Rows 2, 4, 6, 8: Work even.
Row 3: Rep Row 1. 26 sts.

Row 5: Work to m, sm, work 5 sts in patt, ssk, work in patt to 7 sts before m, k2tog, k1, p1, sssk, sm, k1. 22 sts.

Row 7: Work to m, sm, work 5 sts in patt, ssk, work in patt to 5 sts before m, k2tog, work to end. 20 sts.

Row 9: Work to m, sm, work 5 sts in patt, ssk, k5, k2tog, k1, sssk. 16 sts.

Graft the left front and left back shoulder sts together.

FINISHING

Pocket bags:
Remove scrap yarn from pocket and with WS of garment facing, place the resulting 22 sts on dpn. Join yarn and work Reverse St st in the round for 3". Divide sts over 2 needles (11 sts for top of pocket and 11 for bottom) and join using a 3-needle BO.

Pocket trim:
With RS of garment facing, use a tapestry needle to draw ball end of yarn through the fabric from RS to WS at the right edge of the pocket opening. With a single dpn and working left to right using the tail of yarn on the underside of the work, pick up and knit 11 sts from

bottom edge of pocket opening, bringing the loops up through the fabric from WS to RS.

Row 1 (WS): [P1 tbl, k1] to last st, p1 tbl.
Row 2 (RS): [K1 tbl, p1] to last st, k1 tbl.

BO in patt.

Closures (make 3):
With dpn, CO 2 sts and work i-cord for 3" / 7.5cm or until it fits around whatever creep-tastic toggles you've found. Fasten off. Form into a loop and sew to right front edge of vest.

Sew toggle buttons to left edge of vest to correspond with loops.

Weave in ends and block.

Sky Pirates

When stuff on terra firma sucks, some folks will take to
the air. Whether by airship or spaceship, whether gallant
commander or scurvy dog of the stratosphere, these guys
and gals are a rough-and-tumble crowd ... and you can't
take the sky from them.

(... Seriously, don't try.)

Battle Ready

Suesan Roth

To successfully live among the outlaws of the outer rings, you've gotta be tough as nails and twice as sharp. Still, there's no reason to lose your sophistication completely. This vest, inspired by the heroines of the cult favorite *Firefly*, melds "bad ass" with "high class" for a look that will serve you well on all your interplanetary forays, no matter what the 'verse throws at you.

PATTERN NOTES

Vest is worked from the top down, beginning with a yoke shaped using the Contiguous method developed by Susie Myers. After yoke is complete, fronts and back are worked separately to the bottom of the armholes, then stitches are cast on for side panels and vest is worked in one piece to the end of the panels. After side panels are bound off, fronts and back are again worked separately to the hem.

Back and fronts are the same for all sizes; different finished bust sizes are achieved by working wider side panels. Sizing is flexible. The pattern stitch is quite stretchy, and the fronts are not meant to meet across the bust.

Alternate repeats of the stitch pattern on the vest charts are shaded green to aid in following the chart; other than that, the color of a stitch has no particular significance.

Wristlets are worked flat from the top down (fingers to cuff) and closed with lacing.

VEST PATTERN

COLLAR

With smaller needle, CO 105 sts. Work back and forth in rows.

Row 1 (RS): K51, k3tog and place a removable marker in the st just made, k51. 103 sts.
Row 2 (WS): Purl.
Row 3: Knit to 1 st before marked st, k3tog and replace marker in st just made, knit to end. 2 sts dec'd.
Row 4: Purl.
Row 5: Rep Row 3.
Row 6: Knit.
Row 7: Rep Row 3.
Row 8: Purl.
Row 9: Rep Row 3.
Row 10: Knit.
Row 11: Knit to 2 sts before marked st, k5tog and replace marker in st just made, knit to end. 91 sts.
Row 12: Purl.

YOKE

Row 1 (RS): Kfb, k13, pm, k14, pm, knit to 1 st before marked st, k3tog and remove marker, k16, pm, k14, pm, k13, kfb. 91 sts: 15 each front, 14 each shoulder, and 33 for back.
Row 2 (WS): Knit.

Row 3: [Knit to 1 st before m, kfb, sm, knit to next m, sm, kfb] twice, knit to end. 4 sts inc'd.
Row 4: [Purl to 1 st before m, pfb, sm, purl to next m, sm, pfb] twice, purl to end. 4 sts inc'd.

Rows 5–7: Rep Row 3.
Row 8: Rep Row 4.

Rows 9–10: Rep Row 3. 123 sts: 23 each front, 14 each shoulder, and 49 for back.

Row 11 (RS): Knit to m, remove m, [k2tog, transfer 1 st from right needle to left] 15 times, remove m, knit to next m, [k2tog, transfer 1 st from right needle to left] 15 times, remove m, knit to end. 23 sts rem for each front and 49 sts for back.

SIZES

Vest: Women's S (M, L) (see notes); shown in size S

Wristlets: One size

FINISHED MEASUREMENTS

Vest bust: 34.5 (38, 41.5)" / 88 (97, 106)cm

Wristlet circumference: 4.75" / 12cm (unstretched, without laces)

MATERIALS

Malabrigo Arroyo [100% superwash merino; 335 yds / 306m per 100g]; color: Escoria; 6 skeins

40-inch US 2 / 2.75mm circular needle
40-inch US 3 / 3.25mm circular needle

Stitch markers (including 1 removable marker); 3 T-bar toggle necklace clasps; 10–20 yds/m of suede lacing

GAUGE

32 sts and 32 rows = 4" / 10cm in patt st with smaller needles, blocked

28 sts and 40 rows = 4" / 10cm in St st with smaller needles, blocked

Why not make a wristlet to serve as your gauge swatch?

Row 12: Purl right front sts, join a new ball of yarn and purl back sts, join a new ball of yarn and purl left front sts.

Working all parts at the same time with separate balls of yarn, [knit 3 rows, purl 1 row] 4 times, ending with a WS row. Knit 2 rows.

Next row (RS): On left front, kfb, k10, kfb, k10, kfb; on back, kfb, k23, kfb, k23, kfb; on right front, kfb, k10, kfb, k10, kfb. 26 sts each front and 52 sts for back.
Purl 1 row.

Next row (RS): On left front, kfb, k12, m1, k12, kfb; on back, kfb, k25, m1, k25, kfb; on right front, kfb, k12, m1, k12, kfb. 29 sts each front and 55 sts for back.
Knit 1 WS row.

BODY

Working pieces at the same time with separate balls of yarn or one at a time, as preferred, work Rows 1–62 of Left Front, Back, and Right Front charts.

Do not break yarns. You are now at the bottom of the armholes, about to cast on for the side panels.

Row 63 (RS): Work foll chart to last 2 sts of Left Front, pm for side panel, p2; pick up Back, with RS facing use cable method and yarn attached to Back to CO 22 (46, 70) sts, break yarn; use yarn attached to Left Front to work *k2, p2; rep from * to last 2 sts, end k2 over newly CO sts, p2 from Back, pm (counts as first row of Side Panel chart); work foll chart to last 2 sts of Back, pm for side panel, p2; pick up Right Front, with RS facing use cable method and yarn attached to Right Front to CO 22 (46, 70) sts, break yarn; use yarn attached to back to work *k2, p2; rep from * to last 2 sts, end k2 over newly CO sts, p2 from Right Front, pm (counts as first row of Side Panel chart); work foll chart to end of Right Front.

Work following charts as established through Row 100 of Back and Front charts. Change to larger needle.

Work foll charts as established through end of Side Panel chart, which is Row 126 of Back and Front charts. You are now at the level of the side openings, about to bind off the side panels.

Row 127 (RS): Work foll chart across Left Front to m for Side Panel, remove m, join a new ball of yarn, BO 22 (46, 70) Side Panel sts in patt, remove m, work foll chart across Back to m for Side Panel, remove m, join a new ball of yarn, BO 22 (46, 70) Side Panel sts in patt, remove m, work to end.

Working pieces at the same time with separate balls of yarn or one at a time, as preferred, work to end of Back and Front charts. BO all sts in patt on WS.

FINISHING

Weave in ends and wet block. Thread suede lacing through fabric at about hip level, taking care to follow the same row(s) across. Sew on clasps.

WRISTLETS PATTERN

FINGER LOOP

CO 24 sts. BO 24 sts. Do not fasten off last st. Pick up and knit 1 st from opposite end of strip, taking care not to twist it; pass first st on right needle over second. 1 st rem.

Row 1 (RS): K1.
Row 2 (WS): P1.
Row 3: [K1, yo, k1] in same st. 3 sts.
Row 4: Kfb, p1, kfb. 5 sts.
Row 5: Sl 1, k1, psso, k1, k2tog. 3 sts.
Row 6: P3.
Row 7: Sl 1, k2tog, psso. 1 st.
Row 8: P1.

HAND

Work Rows 1–54 of Wristlet chart. BO all sts in patt on RS.

FINISHING

Weave in ends and wet block. Thread suede lacing through eyelet holes.

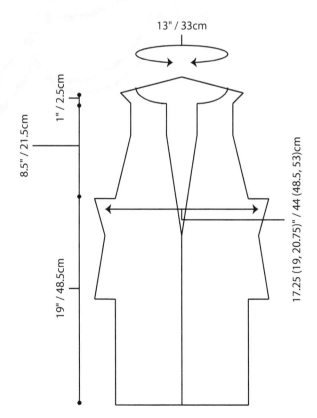

13" / 33cm

1" / 2.5cm

8.5" / 21.5cm

19" / 48.5cm

17.25 (19, 20.75)" / 44 (48.5, 53)cm

Playlist for the End Times

Disclaimer: Some of these songs contain adult language. It is, after all, the apocalypse—a little profanity is to be expected.

- "1999" – Prince
- "Gimme Shelter" – Rolling Stones
- "Calamity Song" – The Decemberists
- "Life During Wartime" – Talking Heads
- "Five Years" – David Bowie
- "It's the End of the World as We Know It" – R.E.M.
- "99 Luftballons" – Nena
- "Black Planet" – Sisters of Mercy
- "The Day the World Went Away" – Nine Inch Nails
- "The Final Countdown" – Europe
- "We Will Become Silhouettes" – The Postal Service
- "Panic" – The Smiths
- "Re: Your Brains" – Jonathan Coulton
- "Bad Moon Rising" – Creedence Clearwater Revival
- "[Nothing But] Flowers" – Talking Heads
- "Nuclear War" – Sun Ra
- "Wake Up and Scream" – Starhole
- "I Melt with You" – Modern English
- "Apocalypse Please" – Muse
- "Invaders Must Die" – The Prodigy
- "Stress" – Justice
- "The Earth Died Screaming" – Tom Waits
- "In the Year 2525" – Zager & Evans

LEFT FRONT

work these 2 rows
a total of 36 times

work these 8 rows
a total of 5 times

157
155
153
151
149
147
145
143
141
139
137
135
133
131
129
127
125
123
121
119
117
115
113
111
109
107
105
103
101
99
97
95
93
91
89
87
85
83
81
79
77
75
73
71
69
67
65
63
61
59
57
55
53
51
49
47
45
43
41
39
37
35
33
31
29
27
25
23
21
19
17
15
13
11
9
7
5
3
1

BACK

work these 2 rows
a total of 44 times

work these 8 rows
a total of 5 times

RIGHT FRONT

work these 2 rows
a total of 36 times

work these 8 rows
a total of 5 times

157
155
153
151
149
147
145
143
141
139
137
135
133
131
129
127
125
123
121
119
117
115
113
111
109
107
105
103
101
99
97
95
93
91
89
87
85
83
81
79
77
75
73
71
69
67
65
63
61
59
57
55
53
51
49
47
45
43
41
39
37
35
33
31
29
27
25
23
21
19
17
15
13
11
9
7
5
3
1

SIDE PANEL

work these 2 rows
a total of 17 times

125
123
121
119
117
115
113
111
109
107
105
103
101
99
97
95
93
91
89
87
85
83
81
79
77
75
73
71
69
67
65
63

Work sts between blue lines for size S

Work sts between pink lines for size M

Work sts between yellow lines for size L

KEY FOR ALL BATTLE READY CHARTS

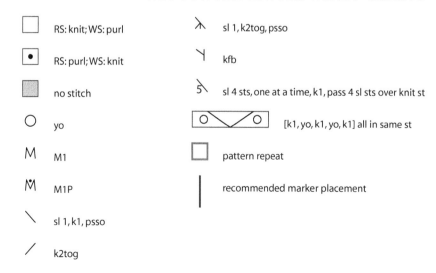

RS: knit; WS: purl

• RS: purl; WS: knit

no stitch

○ yo

M M1

M̈ M1P

\ sl 1, k1, psso

/ k2tog

sl 1, k2tog, psso

kfb

sl 4 sts, one at a time, k1, pass 4 sl sts over knit st

[k1, yo, k1, yo, k1] all in same st

pattern repeat

recommended marker placement

WRISTLET

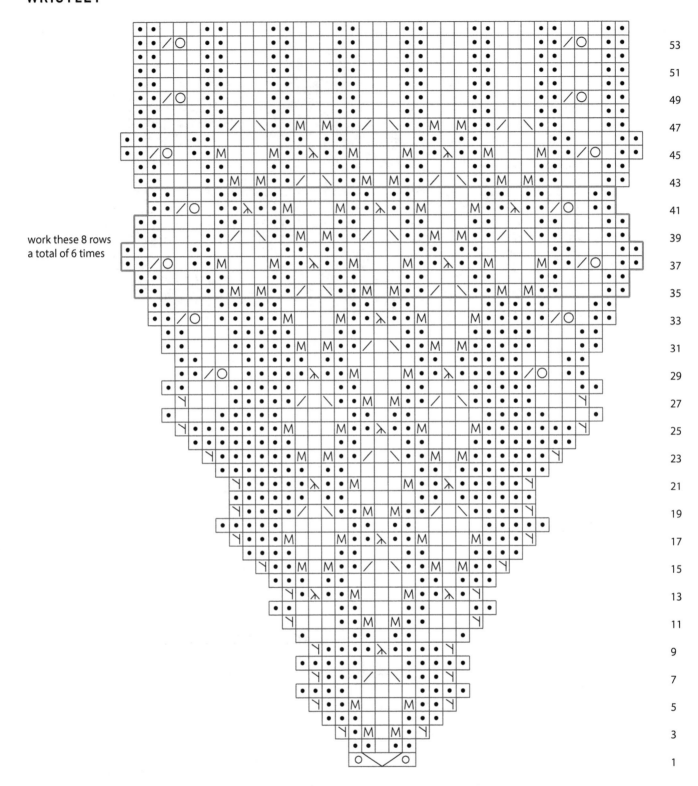

work these 8 rows
a total of 6 times

53

51

49

47

45

43

41

39

37

35

33

31

29

27

25

23

21

19

17

15

13

11

9

7

5

3

1

Oryx

Jennifer Dassau

Easy to slip on over tactical gear or your mesh bralette, Oryx is a drapey tank that is fitted at the bottom with volume at the top and sides—and looks stunning with jodhpurs! Inspired by Margaret Atwood's mysterious character, and knit in a lustrous silk blend yarn, Oryx will haunt the dreams of any survivor.

PATTERN NOTES

This garment is intended to be close fitting at the hem and more drapey at the chest with extra fabric at each side; for a good fit, choose a size based on high hip measurement, and with several inches of positive ease at the bust.

The body of Oryx is knit in the round to the armholes, in stockinette with a purl stripe every tenth round; once the front and back are divided, a 3 stitch garter selvage is worked at the armhole and neck edges to the ends of the shoulder straps.

Bind off underarm and neckline stitches firmly knitwise; one stitch will remain on RH needle after binding off and will be part of the selvage stitch pattern.

After dividing for front and back, slip the first stitch of every row purlwise for a neat edge to the shoulder straps and neckline.

The shoulder straps have working buttons and buttonholes, the placement of which can be adjusted during construction if necessary, and which add to the paramilitary look of the tank. However, due to the very drapey nature of the fabric, invisibly sewing the straps together, as in the sample, may help to make them more secure.

STITCHES AND TECHNIQUES

PURL STRIPE

(Worked in the round)
Knit 9 rnds.
Purl 1 rnd.
Rep these 10 rnds.

(Worked flat)
Rows 1, 3, 5, 7, 9 (WS): Purl.
Rows 2, 4, 6, 8 (RS): Knit.
Row 10 (RS): Purl.
Rep Rows 1–10.

PATTERN

BODY

Using the long-tail method, CO 150 (160 (174, 188, 198, 208, 228, 252, 276) sts. Knit 1 row, pm and join to work in the rnd.

Purl 1 rnd.
Knit 1 rnd.
Rep the last 2 rnds 3 more times.

Next rnd: P75 (80, 87, 94, 99, 104, 114, 126, 138), pm for right side seam, purl to end.

Inc Rnd: [K1, m1R, knit to 1 st before m, m1L, k1, sm] 2 times. 4 sts inc'd.
Knit 8 rnds.
Purl 1 rnd.
Rep the last 10 rnds 9 (9, 9, 9, 9, 10, 10, 10, 10) more times. 190 (200, 214, 228, 238, 252, 272, 296, 320) sts.

SIZES

Women's XXS (XS, S, M, L, XL, 1X, 2X, 3X); shown in size XS

(See Pattern Notes for further information about fit.)

FINISHED MEASUREMENTS

Bust: 38 (40, 42.75, 45.5, 47.5, 50.5, 54.5, 59.25, 64)" / 95 (100, 107, 114, 119, 126, 136, 148, 160)cm

High hip: 30 (32, 34.75, 37.5, 39.5, 41.5, 45.5, 50.5, 55.25)" / 75 (80, 87, 94, 99, 104, 114, 126, 138)cm

MATERIALS

Blue Moon Fiber Arts Marine Silk Fingering (51% silk, 29% merino, 20% Sea Cell rayon; 487 yds / 445m per 100g skein); color: Deep Unrelenting Grey; 2 (2, 3, 3, 3, 3, 4, 4, 4) skeins

24-inch US #5 / 3.75mm circular needle, or size needed to obtain gauge

Stitch markers, two 7/8" / 22mm shank buttons, stitch holder, yarn needle, matching sewing thread and needle

GAUGE

20 sts and 28 rows = 4" / 10 cm in St st
20 sts and 40 rows = 4" / 10 cm in garter stitch

Set up armhole edging:

Note that the Purl Stripe stitch pattern is maintained throughout the entire body, excluding the selvages; the following set-up and dividing rows are Rows/Rnds 1–6 of the Purl Stripe pattern.

Knit 1 rnd.
Next rnd: [P16 (18, 21, 24, 26, 29, 31, 35, 39), k63 (64, 65, 66, 67, 68, 74, 78, 82), p16 (18, 21, 24, 26, 29, 31, 35, 39), sm] 2 times.
Rep the last 2 rnds once more.

Next rnd: Knit, stopping when 13 (15, 18, 21, 23, 26, 28, 32, 36) sts rem before end-of-rnd marker.

Divide front and back:

Next rnd: BO 26 (30, 36, 42, 46, 52, 56, 64, 72) sts, removing m, p2 (3 sts on right needle), k63 (64, 65, 66, 67, 68, 74, 78, 82), p3, and place these 69 (70, 71, 72, 73, 74, 80, 84, 88) sts on holder for front; BO 26 (30, 36, 42, 46, 52, 56, 64, 72) sts, removing side m, p2 (3 sts on right needle), k63 (64, 65, 66, 67, 68, 74, 78, 82), p3. 69 (70, 71, 72, 73, 74, 80, 84, 88) sts rem for back.

UPPER BACK

Purl 1 WS row (counts as Row 7 of Purl Stripe patt).

Dec Row (RS): P3, ssk, knit to last 5 sts, k2tog, p3. 2 sts dec'd.

Maintaining 3 stitch garter selvages (purl every row), rep Dec Row every RS row 6 (6, 6, 6, 6, 6, 8, 9, 10) more times, **at the same time** maintaining Purl Stripe patt. To dec on a RS purl row, work: P3, ssp, purl to last 3 sts, p2tog, p3.

After all decs are complete, 55 (56, 57, 58, 59, 60, 62, 64, 66) sts rem. Work 11 (11, 11, 11, 11, 11, 17, 15, 13) rows even, ending with Row 1 of Purl Stripe patt.

Set up neck edging:

Next row (RS): P3, k13, p23 (24, 25, 26, 27, 28, 30, 32, 34), k13, p3.
Purl 1 row.
Rep these 2 rows once more.

Divide for left and right shoulder:

Next row (RS): P3, k13, p3, join new yarn and BO 17 (18, 19, 20, 21, 22, 24, 26, 28) sts for back neck, p2 (3 sts on right needle after BO), k13, p3. 19 sts rem each shoulder.

Left neck shaping:

Purl 1 WS row (counts as Row 7 of Purl Stripe patt).

Dec Row (RS): P3, ssk, knit to last 3 sts, p3. 1 st dec'd.
Maintaining 3 stitch garter selvages (purl every row), rep Dec Row every RS row 3 more times, **at the same time** maintaining Purl Stripe patt. To dec on a RS purl row, work: P3, ssp, purl to end.

Left shoulder strap:

After all decs are complete, 15 sts rem. Work 36 rows even, ending with Row 10 of Purl Stripe patt.

Purl 2 rows.
Next row (WS): P6, BO 3, purl to end.
Next row: P6, CO 3 sts using backward loop method, purl to end.
Purl 3 rows.

Firmly BO all sts kwise on RS. Cut yarn leaving a 12" / 30cm tail.

Right neck shaping:

Purl 1 WS row (counts as Row 7 of Purl Stripe patt).

Dec Row (RS): P3, knit to last 5 sts, k2tog, p3. 1 st dec'd.
Maintaining 3 stitch garter selvages (purl every row), rep Dec Row every RS row 3 more times, **at the same time** maintaining Purl Stripe patt. To dec on a RS purl row, work: Purl to last 5 sts, p2tog, p3.

Right shoulder strap:

Work same as left strap.

UPPER FRONT

Transfer 69 (70, 71, 72, 73, 74, 80, 84, 88) held front sts to needle and join new yarn with WS facing.

Work same as Upper Back through end of neck shaping (note that "left" and "right" labels will be reversed for Front). 15 sts rem each shoulder.

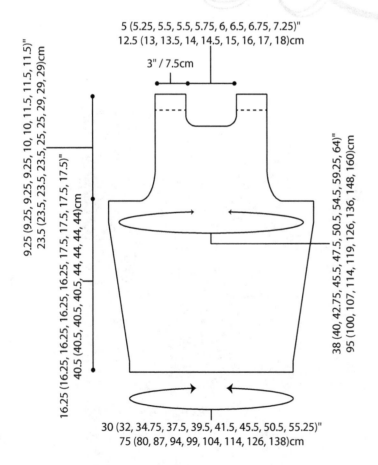

5 (5.25, 5.5, 5.5, 5.75, 6, 6.5, 6.75, 7.25)"
12.5 (13, 13.5, 14, 14.5, 15, 16, 17, 18)cm

3" / 7.5cm

9.25 (9.25, 9.25, 9.25, 10, 10, 11.5, 11.5, 11.5)"
23.5 (23.5, 23.5, 23.5, 25, 25, 29, 29, 29)cm

16.25 (16.25, 16.25, 16.25, 16.25, 16.25, 17.5, 17.5, 17.5)"
40.5 (40.5, 40.5, 40.5, 40.5, 40.5, 44, 44, 44)cm

38 (40, 42.75, 45.5, 47.5, 50.5, 54.5, 59.25, 64)"
95 (100, 107, 114, 119, 126, 136, 148, 160)cm

30 (32, 34.75, 37.5, 39.5, 41.5, 45.5, 50.5, 55.25)"
75 (80, 87, 94, 99, 104, 114, 126, 138)cm

Complete each shoulder strap as foll:
Work 6 (6, 6, 6, 16, 16, 16, 16, 16) rows
even, ending with Row 10 of Purl Stripe
patt.
Purl 7 rows.
Firmly BO all sts kwise on RS. Cut yarn
leaving a 12" / 30cm tail.

FINISHING

Weave in all ends except long tails at
shoulder straps, and steam block. With
yarn or matching sewing thread, sew one
button on each front shoulder strap in
garter section at end of strap. If desired,
once button placement is final, use long
yarn tails and an invisible blind stitch
to sew back and front shoulder straps
securely together. Weave in remaining
ends.

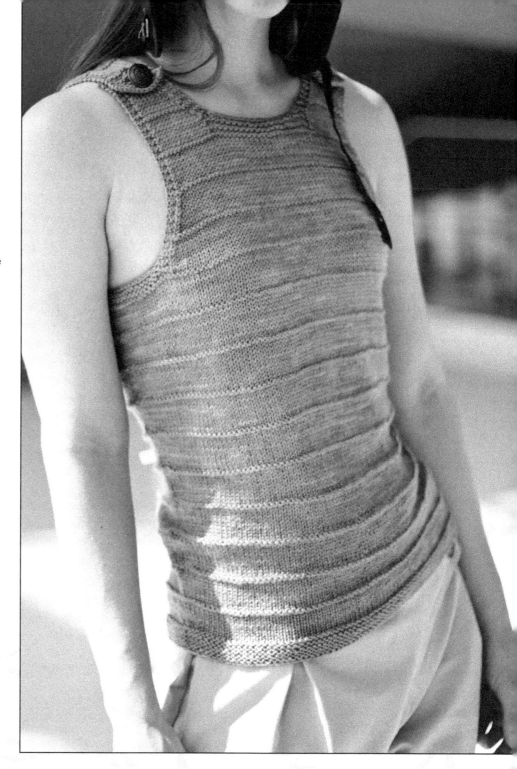

Thrumviator

Michele Lee Bernstein

This thrummed aviator cap begins at the top and increases along four lines, much like the directional winds. The cap is made extra luxe with a touch of silk, and extra warm with thrums, which are bits of fiber worked into the fabric. The earflaps are finished with i-cord tails. You'll be toasty warm despite the chilly upper atmosphere!

STITCHES AND TECHNIQUES

The cap begins with Judy's Magic Cast On, which you can see demonstrated by Judy herself here: <tinyurl.com/judysmco>. If you do not wish to use Judy's Magic Cast On, cast on 12 sts with any other method you like, but you will need to close up the hole in the top of your cap by running the yarn tail through the sts and cinching it shut.

Thrumming is not difficult, but takes quite a bit of ink to explain on paper. Please read the tutorial below, or check out my instructional video: <tinyurl.com/thrummer>.

Unwrap the ball of roving, and tear off a strip about 0.5" / 1.5cm wide. Hold one end between your hands, about 6" / 15cm apart, and pull gently, so that you feel the fibers slip past each other, but not so much that you break it apart. Continue to work your way up the strip, loosening the fibers as you go

(this is called "drafting"). When you've completed your drafting, pull off a piece about 6" / 15cm long (do not cut).

Take the 6" / 15cm strip and fold the ends back towards the center so that they overlap. Roll the center between thumb and forefinger to felt it down a bit. The middle should be about as thick as your yarn, and the thrum should be about 3" / 7.5cm in length. After determining your optimal thrum size, make a stockpile for efficient thrumming.

To knit with a thrum, insert right needle into next st. Wrap thrum around right needle, keeping tails to the back, then work the st as usual, pulling both the st and thrum through. On the following rnd, knit both the thrum and its corresponding st together, through the back loops. Working through the back loop gives the thrum a V-shape on the public side of your work. If you don't work through the back loop, the thrum will appear as a puffy dot, and be less secure. After this second rnd is done, go back and adjust thrums by tugging on the tails one end

at a time to make sure they are even and secure. Thrummed sts are denoted as "t1" in instructions.

Earflaps are worked flat. On the row following the thrumming row, you'll maintain St st by purling the thrum and corresponding st through the back loop.

PATTERN

CAP

With Judy's Magic Cast On, MC, and dpn, CO 12 sts.

Set-up rnd: [K3, pm] 4 times.

Work Rnds 1–41 of Hat chart once, then work Rnds 30–40 again. (Change to 16-inch circular after Rnd 21.) 120 sts.

Work in garter st (knit 1 rnd, purl 1 rnd) for 7 rnds, ending with a knit rnd.

EARFLAPS

Remove markers as you come to them in this round: K18 for right earflap, BO 53 sts for front of cap, k18 for left earflap

SIZE

One size, to fit head circumference up to 24" / 60cm. Due to the nature of the thrum pattern, only one size is given. The lofty thrums will compress to give you a custom fit.

FINISHED MEASUREMENTS

Circumference: 24" / 60cm
Length: 8" / 20.5cm

MATERIALS

Knitted Wit Silky 'n' Plied (60% wool, 40% silk; 225 yds / 206m per 4 oz skein); color: Brown Sugar; 1 skein

Knitted Wit Roving Knot (100% merino wool; 1 oz); color: Natural

16-inch US #7 / 4.5mm circular needle, or size needed to obtain gauge
Set of US #7 / 4.5mm dpns

Stitch markers, yarn needle

GAUGE

20 sts and 28 rnds = 4" / 10 cm in thrummed St st

(19 sts on right needle after BO), BO 29 sts for back of cap. One st remains on right needle; this will be the first st of the right earflap. Earflaps are worked flat.

Right earflap:

Beg with second st (first st is already on your right needle), work Row 1 of Earflap chart.

Work Rows 2–26 of chart. 5 sts rem.

Work i-cord on rem 5 sts for 10" / 25.5 cm. Cut yarn, leaving a 6" / 15cm tail. Using a yarn needle, thread yarn through rem sts and pull tight.

Left earflap:

Replace 19 held sts on needle and join yarn with RS facing. Work Rows 1–26 of Earflap chart. 5 sts rem. Work i-cord as for right earflap.

FINISHING

Weave in all ends. Steam block gently.

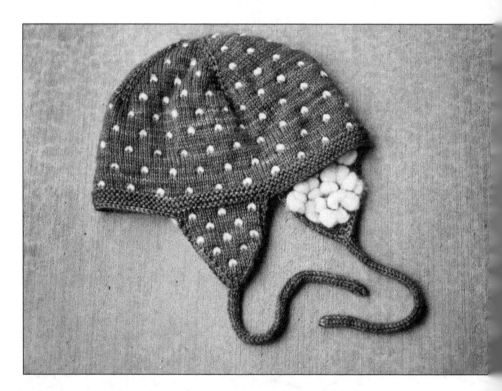

HAT CHART

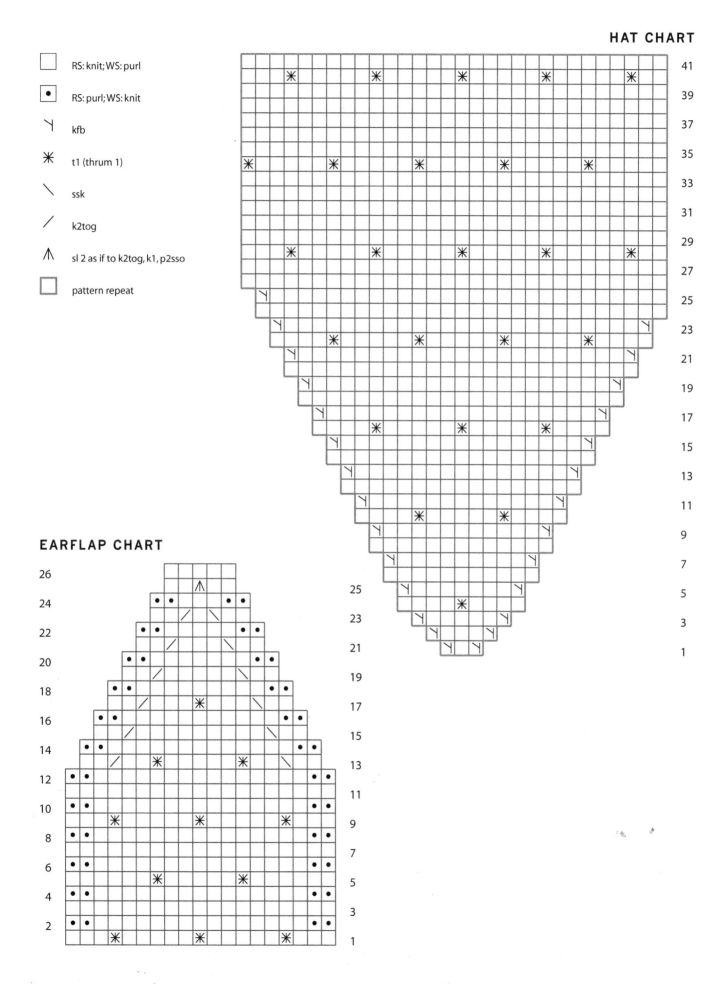

Legend:
- □ RS: knit; WS: purl
- • RS: purl; WS: knit
- ⅄ kfb
- ✳ t1 (thrum 1)
- ╲ ssk
- ╱ k2tog
- ⋀ sl 2 as if to k2tog, k1, p2sso
- ▢ pattern repeat

EARFLAP CHART

WASTELAND VAGABONDS

You know, humans got by just fine as hunter-gatherers for a very long time before we started inventing things like farming and Foursquare. Driven to resourcefulness by the disasters they've endured, some folk will find their way back to the ways of old. Of course, there's not much edible matter left in them thar hills—I suggest you give them a wide berth, lest you find yourself hunted and/or gathered.

RATTLEBONE

Sarah Burghardt

Does the name refer to the ancient instrument, or perhaps the hollow warning of the desperate rattlesnakes that stalk the plains? Are the ridges reminiscent of the prominent ribs of the half-starved and wild-eyed, or perhaps even the eerie spine of an alien queen? Only the Vagabond knows, and you'd be wise not to ask her.

PATTERN NOTES

The mitts are knit top-down, so the sizes can be adjusted as you knit. The mitts shown here have 72 center ridges before starting the cuffs.

In Rnd 1 of the lace panel, there are two yarn overs next to each other. Simply wrap the yarn around the needle twice. On the second row of the lace panel, you will knit the first yarn over and purl the second, creating the ridged backbone effect.

STITCHES AND TECHNIQUES

LACE PANEL

(Worked in the rnd, panel of 18 (22, 26, 30) sts)
Rnd 1: P1, [k2tog, yo] 4 (5, 6, 7) times, [yo, ssk] 4 (5, 6, 7) times, p1.
Rnd 2: P1, k1, [k2tog, yo] 3 (4, 5, 6) times, k1, p1, [yo, ssk] 3 (4, 5, 6) times, k1, p1.
Rep Rnds 1–2.

PATTERN

Using the long tail method, CO 36 (44, 52, 60) sts and join to work in the rnd.

Rnds 1–5: [K1 tbl, p1] to end.

Rnd 6: [K1 tbl, p1] 5 (6, 7, 8) times, k1 tbl, pm for lace panel (LPm), [p1, k1 tbl] 3 (4, 5, 6) times, p1, kfb, [p1, k1 tbl] 3 (4, 5, 6) times, p1, pm for lace panel, [k1 tbl, p1] 5 (6, 7, 8) times. 37 (45, 53, 61) sts.

Rnd 7: Knit to 2 sts before LPm, k2tog, sm, m1p, [k2tog, yo] 4 (5, 6, 7) times, [yo, ssk] 4 (5, 6, 7) times, m1p, sm, ssk, knit to end.

Rnd 8: Knit to LPm, sm, p1, k1, [k2tog, yo] 3 (4, 5, 6) times, k1, p1, [yo, ssk] 3 (4, 5, 6) times, k1, p1, sm, knit to end.

Rnd 9: Knit to LPm, sm, work Rnd 1 of Lace Panel, sm, knit to end.
Rnd 10: Knit to LPm, sm, work Rnd 2 of Lace Panel, sm, knit to end.

Rnds 11–14: Rep Rnds 9–10.
Rnd 15: Rep Rnd 9.

THUMB GUSSETS

Left thumb gusset:
Rnd 16: K2 (3, 3, 4), pm for gusset (Gm), k2, turn work (WS is facing) and use the cable method to CO 12 (14, 14, 16) sts, turn work (RS is facing), k2, pm for gusset, k4 (5, 7, 8), sm, work Rnd 2 of Lace Panel, sm, knit to end.

Rnd 17: [Knit to Gm, sm] 2 times, knit to LPm, sm, work Rnd 1 of Lace Panel, sm, knit to end.

Rnd 18: Knit to Gm, sm, ssk, knit to 2 sts before Gm, k2tog, sm, knit to LPm, sm, work Rnd 2 of Lace Panel, sm, knit to end. 2 sts dec'd.

Rep Rows 17–18 6 (7, 7, 8) more times. 35 (43, 51, 59) sts in total; 2 sts rem between gusset m. Remove gusset m.

Right thumb gusset:
Rnd 16: Knit to LPm, sm, work Rnd 2 of Lace Panel, sm, k4 (5, 7, 8), pm for gusset (Gm), k2, turn work (WS is facing) and use the cable method to CO 12 (14, 14, 16) sts, turn work (RS is facing), k2, pm for gusset, k2 (3, 3, 4).

Rnd 17: Knit to LPm, sm, work Rnd 1 of Lace Panel, sm, [knit to Gm, sm] 2 times, knit to end.

Rnd 18: Knit to LPm, sm, work Rnd 2 of Lace Panel, sm, knit to Gm, sm, ssk, knit to 2 sts before Gm, k2tog, sm, knit to end.

SIZES

S (M, L, XL); shown in size S

To fit forearm circumferences 6 (8, 10, 12)" / 15 (20.5, 25.5, 30.5)cm

FINISHED MEASUREMENTS

Length: 21" / 53.5cm

Forearm circumference: 7 (8.5, 10.25, 11.75)" / 17.5 (21.5, 25.5, 29.5)cm

MATERIALS

Malabrigo Arroyo (100% superwash merino; 335 yds / 306m per 100g skein); color: Glitter; 1 (2, 2, 2) skeins

Set of US #3/3.25mm dpns, or size needed to obtain gauge

3 sets of different colored markers: 1 to mark the end of round, 2 to mark the edges of the lace panel, and 2 to mark the edges of the thumb gusset

Yarn needle

GAUGE

20 sts and 30 rnds = 4" / 10cm in St st

Rep Rows 17–18 6 (7, 7, 8) more times. 35 (43, 51, 59) sts in total; 2 sts rem between gusset m. Remove gusset m.

CUFF

Knit to LPm, sm, work Lace Panel as est, sm, knit to end. Work as est until mitt measures about 2" / 5cm short of desired length, ending after working Rnd 2 of Lace Panel.

UPPER CUFF

Left mitt:

Rnd 1: Knit to LPm, m1, sm, work Rnd 1 of Lace Panel, sm, knit to end. 36 (44, 52, 60) sts.

Right mitt:

Rnd 1: Knit to LPm, sm, work Rnd 1 of Lace Panel, sm, m1, knit to end. Remove end-of-rnd m, p1 tbl, place end-of-rnd m. 36 (44, 52, 60) sts.

Both mitts:

Rnd 2: [K1 tbl, p1 tbl] to end.
Rep the last rnd 13 more times.

PICOT BIND OFF

*Cable CO 3 sts, [k2tog tbl, slip st pwise back to left needle] 5 times; rep from * to end. Cut a 6" / 15cm yarn tail, pass it through a bound off stitch, and through the last live stitch.

FINISHING

Weave in ends. Block gently.

MORE RECOMMENDED READING

☆☆ *Cat's Cradle* by Kurt Vonnegut

Researchers who developed the atomic bomb also developed Ice Nine, an alternative structure for water. It forms a solid, like ice, but doesn't melt. Nothing will ever be the same. —*Rebecca Zicarelli*

☆☆ *Deus Irae* by Phillip K. Dick and Roger Zelazney

World War III happened. Nuclear holocaust. Genetic mutations abound, both in humans and animals. And religion mutates. The Servants of Wrath want a mural of their deity, Carlton Lufteufel, the man who pulled the trigger on Armageddon. And it's up to the painter Tibor McMasters, born without arms or legs, to find Lufteufel and paint his likeness. To me, the most memorable scene in his quest is a gang of intelligent cockroaches worshiping a VW Bug. —*Rebecca Zicarelli*

☆☆ *The Stand* by Stephen King

Seminal post-apocalyptic storytelling, with the usual Stephen King inquisition into Good vs. Evil. There is a hero, a cast of fascinating characters, and all hell finally breaks loose in the sin city of Las Vegas. For those who read the 1978 original novel, it's worth noting that fully one third of the 1990 edition is original material cut from the first publication. —*Jennifer Dassau*

☆☆ *The Passage* by Justin Cronin

It turns out there are vampires living as bats in remote South America, which inspires the U.S. government to create a new secret weapon virus that confers super-immunity. Predictably, the plan goes awry; in a short period of time, most of humanity is wiped out and a superhuman species overruns the earth. The narrative shifts back and forth from the time surrounding the apocalypse and its horrors, to almost a century later where a small community struggles to survive in the long aftermath. The characters are well drawn, and one mysterious little girl spans the entire time frame as the Messiah/Savior. This book is the first in a trilogy which also includes *The Twelve* and a final novel to be released in 2014. —*Jennifer Dassau*

☆ *1984* by George Orwell

Winston hates The Party in secret. He's just old enough to remember a time before the principles of IngSoc ruled the people of Oceania (Britain and the Americas) and still clings to the vague sense that life was better before, that people weren't meant to lead such bleak, narrow lives. As a rectifier in the Ministry of Truth, Winston knows better than most that The Party lies; his job is going back through old newspaper reports and changing them to reflect the present; after all, Big Brother is never wrong. He carries inside himself the desperate hope that someday, one day, he'll be able to contact The Brotherhood, the underground organization that works against The Party in all things. *1984* is a classic of dystopian literature and a sad, beautiful portrait of individuals in a time when the individual no longer matters. —*Jennette Cross*

☆☆ *Brave New World* by Aldous Huxley

Six hundred years after Ford introduced the Model T, he has been raised to god-like status among the Civilized People of Earth. Ford, stability, and happiness are the new religions and the best way to achieve the stability of universal happiness is to make people as homogeneous as possible. People live life from pleasure to pleasure, and for every momentary unhappiness there is soma—a drug with a clean high and no hangover. Babies are made in tubes and raised in special centers where they are conditioned to fit perfectly into their jobs and lives. Bernard, a sleep conditioning specialist, doesn't fit in. There's a rumor that he got too much alcohol in the tube when he was a fetus and he looks and thinks differently from the other Alphas of his class. He takes a lady friend to a Savage Reservation in New Mexico, one of the only places in the world where there aren't Civilized People, and when they return with one of the Savages it throws all London into an uproar. —*Jennette Cross*

☆☆ *Wool* by Hugh Howey

There is only the silo. One hundred and forty four floors, all of them underground, with levels stretching out around the central staircase. Level 1 houses the sheriff's office and holding cell and the Up Top cafeteria. One morning, Sheriff Holston walks into the holding cell, locks himself in, and tells his deputy to get the mayor; he wants to go outside. Outside is dangerous, outside is death, but once you have spoken the desire it is as good as a condemnation; you cannot stay in the silo and risk spreading the poison to others. *Wool* is about families made of comrades, the things we don't say, how far we'll go to find the truth. —*Jennette Cross*

For more reading recommendations, see page 102.

WAYFARER

Jen Lucas

The Wayfarer shawl is knit by making two smaller shawls and then lacing them together for the ultimate in "cobbled together from the wreckage of civilization" chic.

The lace detail on the edging, which is created by working yarnovers on both the right and wrong side of the work, contrasts with the corset-like leather lacing—part "before-times" finery, part après-le-deluge grit.

PATTERN

TRIANGLE 1

CO 6 sts. Knit 2 rows.
Row 1 (RS): K2, yo, knit to last 2 sts, yo, k2. 2 sts inc'd.
Row 2 (WS): K3, yo, purl to last 2 sts, k2. 1 st inc'd.
Rep Rows 1–2 forty-one more times. 132 sts.

Work Rows 1–8 of Lace Chart 3 times. 156 sts.
BO all sts loosely.

TRIANGLE 2

CO 6 sts. Knit 2 rows.
Row 1 (RS): K2, yo, knit to last 2 sts, yo, k2. 2 sts inc'd.
Row 2 (WS): K2, purl to last 3 sts, yo, k3. 1 st inc'd.
Rep Rows 1–2 forty-one more times. 132 sts.

Work Rows 1–8 of Lace Chart 3 times. 156 sts.
BO all sts loosely.

FINISHING

Weave in ends and block using preferred method.

With RS facing up, place the two triangles next to each other such that Triangle 1 is on the right and Triangle 2 is on the left. Using 1/8" ribbon, weave ribbon through the holes created by the yarn overs in corset fashion to seam the two triangles together. Tie ribbon in a knot or bow to secure.

☐	RS: knit; WS: purl
▩	no stitch
⊡	RS: purl; WS: knit
○	yo
╱	RS: k2tog; WS: p2tog
⟋	RS: p2tog; WS: k2tog
☐	pattern repeat

LACE CHART

SIZE

One size

FINISHED MEASUREMENTS

Wingspan: 52" / 132cm
Depth: 24" / 61cm

MATERIALS

String Theory Caper Sock (80% superwash merino wool, 10% cashmere, 10% nylon; 400 yds / 366m per 113g skein); color: Brina; 1 skein

24-inch US #4 / 3.5mm circular needle, or size needed to obtain gauge

Yarn needle, 6 yds / 5.5m of 1/8" / 3mm wide ribbon

GAUGE

18 sts and 28 rows = 4" / 10cm in St st

Gauge is not critical in this pattern, but a different gauge will affect amount of yarn used and size of finished item.

FORAGER

Alexandra Tinsley

You know, "I've been wandering around the desolate plains" can be a good look! Crisp crepe-y silk is cool in the heat and warm in the cold, and the simple shape and large gauge knit up quickly. The detached cowl adds additional warmth or protection from the sun (or prying eyes.)

PATTERN NOTES

Vest consists of three pieces: back, left front, and right front. Each piece is knit flat, then seamed, leaving openings for armholes. Cowl is worked in the round.

VEST PATTERN

BACK

CO 47 (56, 65, 74, 83) sts. Do not join. Work in St st for 22 (23, 24, 25, 26)" / 56 (58.5, 61, 63.5, 66)cm. BO.

LEFT FRONT

CO 25 (30, 35, 40, 45) sts. Work in St st for 22 (23, 24, 25, 26)" / 56 (58.5, 61, 63.5, 66)cm, ending with a WS row.

Short row shaping:
Row 1 (RS): K20 (25, 30, 34, 38), w&t.
Row 2 and all WS rows: Purl.
Row 3: K16 (20, 24, 27, 31), w&t.
Row 5: K12 (15, 18, 20, 23), w&t.
Row 7: K8 (10, 12, 14, 16), w&t.
Row 9: K4 (5, 6, 7, 8), w&t.
Row 11: Knit to end, picking up wraps and knitting them tog with wrapped sts. BO.

RIGHT FRONT

CO 42 (50, 58, 66, 74) sts. Work in St st for 22 (23, 24, 25, 26)" / 56 (58.5, 61, 63.5, 66)cm, ending with a RS row.

Short row shaping:
Row 1 (WS): P38 (45, 53, 60, 67), w&t.
Row 2 and all RS rows: Knit.
Row 3: P34 (40, 47, 53, 60), w&t.
Row 5: P29 (35, 41, 46, 53), w&t.
Row 7: P25 (30, 35, 40, 45), w&t.
Row 9: P21 (25, 30, 33, 38), w&t.
Row 11: P16 (20, 24, 27, 30), w&t.
Row 13: P12 (15, 18, 20, 23), w&t.
Row 15: P8 (10, 12, 14, 16), w&t.
Row 17: P4 (5, 6, 7, 8), w&t.
Row 19: Purl to end, picking up wraps and purling them tog with wrapped sts. BO.

FINISHING

Place back piece flat, RS down. Place front pieces on top of it, RS up, with the shorter edges to the sides and the longer edges in the center (they will overlap). The top edges of the fronts should match up with the top edge of the back, but the bottom edges will be longer.

Measure 7 (8, 9, 10, 11)" / 18 (20.5, 23, 25.5, 28)cm down from the shoulder and mark with a safety pin or removable stitch marker. Using mattress stitch, seam from that point down to the bottom on each side. Seam from the outside edge of the shoulder inwards 4.5 (5, 5.5, 6, 6.5)" / 11.5 (12.5, 14, 15, 16.5)cm on each side, leaving the center open for the neck.

Weave in all ends and block gently.

COWL PATTERN

CO 45 sts, place marker A, CO 45 more sts, place marker B (beg-of-rnd marker) and join to work in the round. Work in St st for 15.5" / 39.5cm.

Next rnd: Knit to 1 st before marker A, yo, k1, sm, k1, yo, knit to end. 2 sts inc'd.
Knit 1 rnd.
Rep these 2 rnds 7 more times. 106 sts.

BO.
Weave in ends and block gently.

SIZES

Women's XS (S, M, L, XL); shown in size S

Intended to be worn with 0–3" / 0–7.5cm of positive ease. Because of the nature of this fabric, the sizing is extremely flexible.

FINISHED MEASUREMENTS

Bust: 30 (36, 42, 48, 54)" / 75 (90, 105, 120, 135)cm

Cowl: 19.25" / 48.5cm tall and 30" / 75cm in circumference

MATERIALS

Shibui Heichi (100% silk; 105 yds / 96m per 50g skein); color: Steel; 4 (5, 6, 8, 9) skeins for vest; 3 skeins for cowl

24-inch US #10.75 / 7mm circular needle, or size needed to obtain gauge

Removable markers or safety pins, yarn needle, shawl pin or brooch (optional)

GAUGE

12 sts and 17.5 rows = 4" / 10 cm in St st

This yarn, when worked at a loose gauge, has a tendency to be amorphous. As long as your gauge is in the right neighborhood you are probably okay, given the flexible nature of the garment.

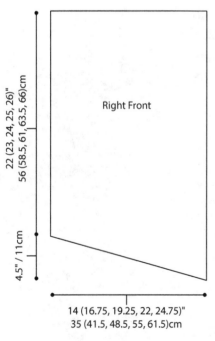

Right Front

22 (23, 24, 25, 26)"
56 (58.5, 61, 63.5, 66)cm

4.5" / 11cm

14 (16.75, 19.25, 22, 24.75)"
35 (41.5, 48.5, 55, 61.5)cm

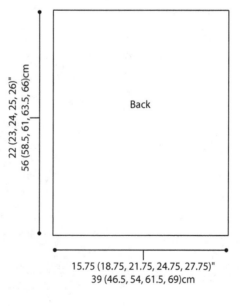

Back

22 (23, 24, 25, 26)"
56 (58.5, 61, 63.5, 66)cm

15.75 (18.75, 21.75, 24.75, 27.75)"
39 (46.5, 54, 61.5, 69)cm

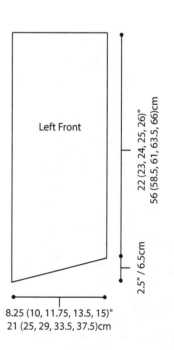

Left Front

22 (23, 24, 25, 26)"
56 (58.5, 61, 63.5, 66)cm

2.5" / 6.5cm

8.25 (10, 11.75, 13.5, 15)"
21 (25, 29, 33.5, 37.5)cm

10 THINGS YOU MIGHT NOT REALIZE YOU CAN EAT

('CAUSE POST-APOCALYPTIC BEGGARS CAN'T BE CHOOSERS!)

⚶ Pretty much any mammal or bird

There are a few poisonous birds in Papua New Guinea, but most of 'em are good eatin'. Rats can carry diseases that make them inadvisable as a dish, but rabbits, squirrels, and opossums are good to go. Cook everything extremely well to kill pathogens (and handle with gloves if at all possible, especially if it's a rabies-carrying species.) Buzzards and vultures are said to be pretty nasty tasting and are probably worth a pass. Oh, and avoid the liver of carnivores, as it can give you an overdose of Vitamin A.

⚶ Black walnuts

Just makes sure they're fully shelled and nothing's been chewing on them.

⚶ Cattails

The roots, shoots, and even the pollen are edible. Make sure it's got that weird corn-dog looking bit, though—there are other plants that can look similar that are no good.

⚶ Bugs!

Not all of them, but carpenter ants, bee larvae, cicadas, crickets, earthworms, grasshoppers, junebugs, and mealworms are all good eatin'. Pill bugs (aka "roly-polies") are actually land-dwelling relatives of lobsters and apparently even turn red when boiled. (We have not verified that tidbit, though.)

⚶ Snakes

If it's a venomous snake, cut off the head (being very careful—their reflexes can strike even after they're dead!), and bury it so that you won't step on it. Apparently they smell pretty foul, but the meat is edible once cooked!

⚶ The eggs of almost anything

Collecting wild bird eggs is illegal in most countries, but after civilization is destroyed, it's probably OK. The eggs of any bird are safe to eat at just about any stage (except maybe the aforementioned birds in Papua New Guinea.) Unlaid eggs from inside an animal that you've killed are also fair game. Turtle, alligator, snake, and iguana eggs are edible, but watch out for mama! Some fish eggs are very edible but some toxic, so skip those unless you're confident in your ability to tell the difference.

⚶ Queen Anne's Lace

Also called Wild Carrot, because, um, it's a carrot! The catch: you have to find it before the flower blooms or the root will be woody (though you can peel it off and eat the inside), and it's easy to mistake for toxic hemlock.

⚶ Dandelions

Forget dandelion wine. (This is no time to get drunk! There could be zombies!) You can eat the roots and leaves as well. They are a little bitter, though taste better before the flowers appear.

⚶ Prickly pear cacti

You know those cactuses with the thick, flat, oval-shaped "pads"? Yeah, you can eat those, or turn them into jam. They apparently taste kind of like asparagus, and the young ones are said to be tastiest. The fruit and flower are also edible. Just watch the spines! Wear gloves and peel it thoroughly.

⚶ Stinging nettle

I know, sounds like a horrible idea, right? But as soon as you cook these nettles, they lose their sting, and have a ton of protein and vitamins. Just make sure you're wearing gloves for the first part.

And thus we come to the end of the end. We hope you've enjoyed this fanciful ride as much as we have—almost as much as we hope you won't start blowing anything up or conducting horrible experiments that end in plagues and zombies. (May I suggest doing some knitting, instead?)

Good luck, godspeed, and duck and cover!

ABBREVIATIONS

approx	approximately
beg	begin, beginning
BO	bind off
CC	contrasting color
ch	chain
cn	cable needle
CO	cast on
cont	continue / continuing
dec / dec'd	decrease / decreased
dpn(s)	double-pointed needle(s)
est	established
foll	following
inc / inc'd	increase / increased
k	knit
k2tog	right-leaning decrease: knit 2 sts together as one
k3tog	right-leaning decrease: knit 3 sts together as one
kfb	knit into front and back of a single st (increase)
kwise	knitwise, as if to knit
LLI	left lifted increase: knit into the right leg of the st two rows below last st on right needle
m	marker
m1 / m1L	use left needle tip to lift strand between sts from front to back; knit this loop through the back loop
m1LP	use left needle tip to lift strand between sts from front to back; purl into back of this new stitch
m1p / m1RP	use left needle tip to lift strand between sts from back to front; purl this loop
m1R	use right needle tip to lift strand between sts from back to front; knit this loop
MC	main color
mult	multiple
p	purl
p2tog	purl 2 sts together as one
p3tog	purl 3 sts together as one
patt	pattern

pfb	purl into front and back of a single st (increase)
pm	place marker
psso	pass slipped st over
pwise	purlwise, as if to purl
rem	remain(s)/remaining
rep	repeat
RLI	right lifted increase: knit into the left leg of the st below next st on left needle
rnd(s)	round(s)
RS	right side
s2kp	slip 2 sts together knitwise, k1, pass slipped st over
sc	single crochet
skp	slip 1 st knitwise, k1, pass slipped st over
sl	slip
sm	slip marker
ssk	left-leaning decrease: slip 2 sts knitwise one at a time, then knit them together through the back loop
ssp	[with yarn in front, slip 1 knitwise] twice; return 2 sts to left needle, then purl 2 together through the back loop, inserting right needle through bottom st first
sssk	left-leaning decrease: slip 3 sts knitwise one at a time, then knit them together through the back loop
st(s)	stitch(es)
St st	stockinette (stocking) stitch
tbl	through the back loop
tog	together
w&t	wrap and turn ⚠ On a knit or RS row: Sl next st pwise wyib, bring yarn to front, return sl st to left needle, turn work. ⚠ On a purl or WS row: Sl next st pwise wyif, bring yarn to back, return sl st to left needle, turn work.
WS	wrong side
wyib	with yarn in back
wyif	with yarn in front
yo	yarn over

TECHNIQUES

Turkish CO
Easier demonstrated than explained: bit.ly/18DOm5d

3-needle BO
Have the two sets of sts to be joined on separate needles, held together in the left hand with right sides facing each other (unless otherwise specified). With a spare needle, insert needle into first st on front needle, then first st on back needle and knit both sts together. *Insert needle into next st on front needle, then next st on back needle and knit both sts together. Pass first st on right needle over second to BO 1 st. Rep from *.

Crochet cast on
⚶ Step 1: Make a slip stitch and place it on the crochet hook.
⚶ Step 2: Hold the knitting needle in the left hand and the hook in the right. Bring the yarn around the back of the needle.
⚶ Step 3: Using the hook, lift a loop of yarn over the top of the needle, making the first stitch, and pull it through the stitch on the hook.
⚶ Step 4: Move the yarn around behind the needle.

Rep steps 2–4 until one fewer than the required number of sts are on the needle. Place the stitch on the hook onto the needle.

I-cord
(Worked on two dpns over a small number of sts.)
Knit to end of row. Do not turn work. Slide sts to other end of dpn, bring yarn firmly across back of work. Rep from *.

ABOUT THE DESIGNERS

ALEXANDRA "HOW I STOPPED WORRYING AND LEARNED TO LOVE THE YARN" TINSLEY

Alex lives in Michigan with too many dogs. She likes ducklings and sandwich cookies, but not for the same purpose. When the apocalypse comes, she'll either be the first to go, or the very ironic last one standing. Her website is www.dull-roar.com, and you can find her on Ravelry as alextinsley and on Twitter @alex_tinsley.

BRENDA "PATIENT ZERO" K. B. ANDERSON

Brenda K. B. Anderson makes mascots during the day. She cooks, knits, crochets, and bellydances at night. Brenda lives in a little house in Saint Paul, Minnesota, with her ridiculously good-looking husband and their hairy baby, Mr. Kittypants. She answers to yarnville on Ravelry.

RACHEL "DEVOURED BY ZOMBIES" ANDERSON

Rachel (Tomyris on Ravelry) teaches mathematics and Knitting For Self-Defense (Protection from the Elements 101) in Ireland's wettest county. She plans to avoid the Apocalypse completely—zombie sheep permitting—by living in a rural wilderness and growing her own heritage potatoes. She blogs infrequently at thornmaiden.wordpress.com, weather permitting.

FLOSSIE "SHOT A MANDROID IN RENO JUST TO WATCH HIM DIE" AREND

Flossie Arend loves all things sci-fi-, horror-, and geek-related, so being a part of this project is a dream come true. A writer by trade, much of her time is spent reading, writing, and knitting at home. You can see more of her work at flossieknits.com or on Ravelry, Twitter, and Facebook as flossieknits.

ANNIKA "MAD SCIENTIST" BARRANTI

Annika Barranti is preparing for the apocalypse in Los Angeles, where her stockpile of woolens does not often come in handy now, but will in the Nuclear Winter. Or so she hopes. You can find Annika at her personal website, noirbettie.com, her knitting website, noirknits.com, and on Ravelry, Twitter, and the rest of the internet as noirbettie.

MICHELE "IT WAS EARTH ALL ALONG" LEE BERNSTEIN

Michele has been knitting since her Aunt Rose taught her when she was 14, but became a knit-fiend when she joined a knitting group, Ravelry, and started knit-blogging in the past few years. She is particularly fond of texture (cables and lace) and learning new techniques (entrelac, thrumming, and steeking are her current favorites). She loves teaching people how to be the boss of their knitting! You can view her blog and patterns at pdxknitterati.com and find her on Ravelry and Twitter as pdxknitterati.

Twist Collective, Interweave, and others. Visit ravelry.com/designers/sharon-fuller on Ravelry to see more of her work.

ELLEN "ATE RADIOACTIVE FISH AND GREW A" GILL

Ellen Gill is a British designer who picked up the needles at the tender age of 21 and has been knitting at a furious (and frankly, unreasonable) rate ever since. When civilization finally collapses, she will be found in her secret bunker with her stockpile of gin and a set of 2.25mm metal dpns for self-defense. Her Ravelry name is Melonby and she also blogs at apileofsheep.wordpress.com

MELISSA "BAD-ASS DISTRICT 1 TRIBUTE" LEMMONS

Melissa Lemmons has been getting ready for the apocalypse from a young age by reading lots of fantasy literature and improving her needlework skills. Between the spinning, knitting, and sharp needles, she and her family will be safe and warm. Her website is melissalemmonsdesigns.com and she is on Ravelry as Knitterleigh.

JEN "READ ALOUD FROM THAT CURSED BOOK" LUCAS

Jen Lucas has been knitting since 2004 and designing since 2008. When not knitting, Jen can be found in a lab testing raw sewage. She dreams of being featured on the TV show *Dirty Jobs with Mike Rowe*. Want to see what else Jen has been designing? Check out her website jenlucasdesigns.com or find her on Ravelry as jenlucas.

AMY "DREAMING OF ELECTRIC SHEEP" MANNING

Amy Manning lives in Phoenix, Arizona, with her husband and talented cat, Tuna Breath. She makes art, knits, crochets, sews. You can find her online at frogesan.tumblr.com and republicofyarn.blogspot.com. Her Ravelry name is Lizardman.

SARAH "SINGLE-HANDEDLY RESPONSIBLE FOR GLOBAL WARMING" BURGHARDT

Sarah Burghardt is inspired by texture, color, and shape, and is always on the lookout for interesting construction. She also has a passion for choral folk music, especially from the Republic of Georgia.

JENNETTE "SENT TO THE ATTIC" CROSS

Jennette is hoping the end of the world is more nuclear winter than desert wasteland, and that after it all goes down someone will be looking to hire a knitter who loves stories, especially science fiction, fantasy, fairy tales, and mysteries. There's more call for storytellers huddled around a campfire. Her favorite apocalypse is the Thoughtpocalypse from *Dollhouse*. If you wish to challenge

her to a Whedon Trivia Showdown, you can find her as doviejay on Ravelry and Twitter or at doviejayknits.com

JENNIFER "CHICKIENOB" DASSAU

Jennifer Dassau is a recovering attorney and emigree from 7th Avenue, who now combines the technical and creative to design knitwear. She blogs in The Knitting Vortex at jenniferdassau.com, and can be found on Ravelry as knittingvortex.

SHARON "THOUGHT THE ALIENS WERE KIND OF CUTE" FULLER

Sharon works as a database developer and enjoys designing knitting patterns as another sort of programming. Sharon is a frequent contributor to Cooperative Press publications, and has designed for

MARA "BOMB-RIDER" MARZOCCHI

Mara Marzocchi (Ares on Ravelry) knits incessantly, mostly socks. She lives in Woburn, Massachusetts, with her large-footed husband and her sadly sockless dog.

RHIANNON "CUNNING HAT" MCCULLOCH

Rhiannon McCulloch has a BA Hons in Fashion Design from Central Saint Martins in London. She is a British Bridal Awards winner, London Marketing Society future fashion award winner and a featured designer in London's Jeans For Genes Day. Amongst other things, she has experience as a stylist/designer on music videos, boutique designer/pattern cutter, couture bridalwear designer and has shown at Alternative London Fashion Week. She currently works as an Art, Illustration and Knit Design teacher and hand knit designer. She is a lifelong knitter and her work is regularly published by *Knit Now* magazine and has appeared in *Yarnwise Magazine*. She self-publishes through Theatre Of Yarns (theatreofyarns.com) and is currently obsessed with the launch of Stitch Seekers (stitchseekers.com), a bi-annual, high fashion, knit and crochet pattern publication.

MICHELE "THE SKY IS FALLING!" MOSKALUK

Michele is a life-long fiber enthusiast. She learned to crochet as a child and taught herself to knit in college. Althought she loves mid-century designs and apparel, Michele is constantly on the lookout for new and interesting techniques to inspire her. Michele currently lives in New England, with an ever growing fiber flock, and sells yarn at bbandbsheep.com

HOLLY "TEENAGE MUTANT NINJA" PRIESTLEY

Holly, The SillyLittleLady, has been knitting and designing since she was in the single digits. She enjoys the mathematical and puzzle-like qualities of this post-apocalyptic life skill. When not knitting, she can be found running, cooking and enjoying a tasty beverage. Find more of her work at sillylittlelady.com.

SUESAN "DID, IN FACT, START THE FIRE" ROTH

Suesan Roth likes to design outside of the box so to speak: "I just truly enjoy trying to find different ways to do the same garment—it's like being a kid again where your only limit is your imagination." Her work has been in *Jane Austen Knits*, Knit Picks, *Quick & Simple Knit Hats & Scarves: 14 Designs from Up-and-Coming Designers!*, Malabrigo Quickies, and will be in a few more books to come. She was also a finalist in the 2013 NY Vogue Knitting design contest.

JOANNE "DOC MARTENS AND ATTITUDE" SCRACE

Joanne Scrace (aka Not So Granny) specializes in seamless knitting and crochet, often vintage inspired but always with a fresh modern feel. She blogs about this and the trials of mixing kids and knitting needles at notsogranny.blogspot.com. Find her on Ravelry at ravelry.com/designers/joanne-scrace

THERESSA "ALL I WANT TO DO IS EAT YOUR BRAINS" SILVER

Theressa loves the mathematical and technical aspects of knitting and is inspired by the physical characteristics of knit fabrics to test the limits and create the unexpected. She lives in Oregon with her husband, son, five cats, and a dog who all participate one way or another in the knitting process.

About the Photographer

Two of Vivian Aubrey's great loves in life are light and wool, so of course she loves nothing better than photographing yarn and knitting. She lives in the thriving craft culture of the Pacific Northwest with her family and specializes in knitwear and portrait photography. You can see her work at vivianaubrey.com.

"TOXIC WASTE SPILL"-YJANE

Jane lives in a 100-year-old house in Windsor, Ontario, that she shares with her husband and a stuffed pheasant named Phileas. When not knitting she usually can be found upended in her extensive cottage gardens. She believes that gardening—like knitting—is a useful post-apocalyptic skill.

KATHERINE "ROCKATANSKY" VAUGHAN

Katherine Vaughan has been knitting for 25+ years and designing for more than five. She primarily designs children's wear and accessories for adults and the home. An avid reader, she particularly enjoys post-apocalyptic and speculative fiction, with a recent interest in zombie lit. Katherine daylights as an academic librarian in Virginia, where it is sometimes cold enough to wear her handknits. Website: ktlvdesigns.com. Ravelry: KTLV

ALEXANDRA "DOOMSDAY DEVICE" VIRGIEL

Alexandra designs and tech edits from her home in Iowa. She can be found online at alexandravirgiel.com and on Ravelry as virgiel.

REBECCA "AND I FEEL FINE" ZICARELLI

Rebecca Zicarelli lives and knits in mountains of Western Maine. Her patterns and projects are on Ravelry under RebeccaZicarelli. She can be found knitting most Tuesday afternoons with the knitting circle at A Wrinkle in Thyme Farm in Sumner, Maine; you're welcome to join if you're in the neighborhood.

Acknowledgments

We have a lot of people to thank for helping bring 'round the end of the world.

First, a huge thank you to all of the designers for lending your fabulous talents and support.

Thanks to Shannon Okey and everyone who makes Cooperative Press go round.

Thank you to Vivian Aubrey Photography (and to Anaiah for her considerable patience).

A major thanks to our models, Katy, Emily, Ruby, and Kelsy for bravely bearing bad weather, skimpy outfits, and inexpertly wielded makeup brushes.

Thank you to Evergreen Aviation Museum and Satsop Business Park for allowing us to use their sites.

Many thanks to our awesome yarn company sponsors (listed at right).

And of course a HUGE thank you all of our Kickstarter supporters, without whom this would have been impossible.

And on a personal note, thank you to the friends and family that have supported/put up with me during this project, and Travis in particular.

YARN SPONSORS

Berroco Fine Handknitting Yarns
berroco.com

Black Trillium Fibre Studio
blacktrilliumfibres.com

Blue Moon Fiber Arts
bluemoonfiberarts.com

Blue Sky Alpacas
blueskyalpacas.com

Cephalopod Yarns
cephalopodyarns.com

Donegal Yarns
donegalyarns.com

Dream in Color Yarns
dreamincoloryarn.com

Jelly Yarns
jellyyarns.com

Knit Collage
knitcollage.com

Knitted Wit
etsy.com/shop/KnittedWit

Knitting Fever (Elsebeth Lavold)
knittingfever.com

Lorna's Laces
lornaslaces.net

Madelinetosh
madelinetosh.com

Malabrigo
malabrigoyarn.com

Play at Life Fiber Arts
playatlifefiberarts.com

Quince & Co.
quinceandco.com

Shibui Knits
shibuiknits.com

Skacel Collection, Inc.
skacelknitting.com

Skeinz
skeinz.com

String Theory Yarn
stringtheoryyarn.com

The Unique Sheep
theuniquesheep.com

About Cooperative Press

Cooperative Press (formerly anezka media) was founded in 2007 by Shannon Okey, a voracious reader as well as writer and editor, who had been doing freelance acquisitions work, introducing authors with projects she believed in to editors at various publishers.

Although working with traditional publishers can be very rewarding, there are some books that fly under their radar. They're too avant-garde, or the marketing department doesn't know how to sell them, or they don't think they'll sell 50,000 copies in a year.

5,000 or 50,000. Does the book matter to that 5,000? Then it should be published.

In 2009, Cooperative Press changed its named to reflect the relationships we have developed with authors working on books. We work together to put out the best quality books we can and share in the proceeds accordingly.

Thank you for supporting independent publishers and authors. Join our mailing list for information on upcoming books!

CPSIA information can be obtained
at www.ICGtesting.com
Printed in the USA
JSHW010553120520
5619JS00003B/7

9 781937 513375